COWHAND

Books by the same author

HOUND-DOG MAN

THE HOME PLACE

FABULOUS EMPIRE

COWHAND:

THE STORY OF A WORKING COWBOY

BY FRED GIPSON

HARPER & BROTHERS PUBLISHERS
NEW YORK

COWHAND: *The Story of a Working Cowboy*

Copyright, 1948, 1953, by Fred Gipson
Printed in the United States of America

FIRST EDITION

G-C

Library of Congress Catalog Card No. 53–7734

AUTHOR'S NOTE

THIS is the true story of a West Texas cowhand. That it turned out to be the story of a "typical" cowhand, is, for me, purely incidental. I gathered Ed Alford's stories because his are the kind I like. I am, by profession and by nature, a collector and writer of tales, and, for me, a good tale, well told, is enough. It doesn't need to prove or signify anything. But since my friend Ed, better known as "Fat," is probably as representative a cowboy as can be found anywhere, perhaps the reader may know more about all real cowboys when he has read the tales of this one.

By Hollywood standards, Fat is a far cry from being a typical cowhand. He never shot a man in his life. He never chased a rustler across the Rio Grande. He never rescued a beautiful girl from ruthless bandits and rode off into the sunset with his arm about her waist. He never carved a cattle empire out of a "howling wilderness."

The truth is, he doesn't even look like a cowboy. He's too squat and heavy; he's too short-legged and bull-necked. He's so potbellied and yet so hipless that some consider it a minor miracle that his pants aren't forever slipping down to hang around his hocks. It is very doubtful that he could hire on as a Hollywood extra in the quickest of quickie Westerns.

But, in ranch country, when a cowman sets out to

hire help, he's not much concerned with a man's sex appeal or photogenic qualities; what he's looking for is a man who can get the job done, a *working* cowhand. And Fat Alford is that.

He can rope a cow out of a brush patch so thick that a Hollywood cowboy couldn't crawl into it on his hands and knees. He can break a horse for riding, doctor a wormy sheep, make a balky gasoline engine pump water for thirsty cattle, tail up a winter-poor cow, or punch a string of post holes across a rocky ridge. He can make out with patched gear, sorry mounts, and skimpy grub, and still get the job done. He can do it in freezing weather or under a sun "hot enough to raise blisters on a boot heel." And all the time, under any circumstances, he works with the thorough understanding that it's the livestock that counts, not the cowhand.

On top of all this, he's got a quality common to most working cowhands: a way of meeting life head on, with a recklessness and a wildness of spirit and a real relish for conquering it. He goes after life as if it were something that had to be roped in a hurry before it got away. And whether he catches it or not, it's a good chase, worth the try, and will make an entertaining yarn to tell the next time he runs into somebody like me.

FRED GIPSON

COWHAND

COWHAND

1

LIKE many a cowhand who has spent a lifetime in the saddle, Fat Alford didn't set out in the beginning with any full-grown notion of becoming one. He just sort of drifted into the work, mainly on account of his aversion to a cotton patch.

Born in 1901 of parents who rent-farmed for a living in both Texas and Oklahoma, little Eddy, as he was called at first, got his fill of cotton growing and cotton picking long before he was old enough to do anything about it. For "thirteen months out of every year," he was breaking cotton land, planting cotton seed, chopping cotton, hoeing weeds out of cotton, and picking cotton.

The picking was the worst. For a spirited boy whose chunky body cried out for action and excitement, cotton picking was backbreaking, soul-killing drudgery. The hot sun blistered the skin on Fat's neck. He'd crawl till he wore his knees raw, then stand bent over till his back ached and the blood ran to his head and hammered at the top of his skull with each pulse beat. Salty sweat would sting his eyes; the cotton burrs would prick his fingers till they were raw. And, snatch at the white fluffy lint and stuff it in his sack as fast as he could, he always came out with the same results when weighing time came. Just about every cotton picker in the field had picked more pounds than he had.

By the time he was fourteen, Fat had made up his mind about one thing: he didn't know exactly just what he aimed to do for the rest of his life, but it sure wasn't going to be cotton growing.

He started looking around, picking up any sort of odd job he could get—hay raking, corn pulling, herding sheep for an old man at Talpa, Texas, working as a spare hand during roundup time for Hubert Woodard, who ran a cow outfit on the Colorado River near Valera. Anything to keep him out of the cotton patch.

Of it all, he liked best to ride for the cow outfit. Things happened, once he mounted a horse. There was action, excitement. Of even greater importance was what happened to *him*. On the ground, standing on his short bandy legs, he felt less than other men; but mounted, he felt the equal of any. A cowhand maybe didn't make a lot more money than a cotton picker; but he sure didn't have to work on his bent knees, with his head bowed and his back aching and his sight and imagination limited to the narrow strip of bare ground between two rows of cotton stalks. A cowhand worked from the back of a horse, where he could hold his head high and look as far out across the country as his eye was good.

Fat didn't have the knowledge of history to tell him that, throughout the ages, the man on a horse has been the man respected and honored by the man afoot. All he knew was that, once he was mounted, his spirit came alive, his imagination soared.

When, in November of 1916, Fat learned that the Hardin brothers, in the southern part of Coleman County, were fixing to move some cattle down into the

2

Juno country on Devil's River, he hurried off down there, hit them up for a riding job—and got it.

The Hardins were named Chris and John. Chris bossed the outfit and knew his business. Fat remembers him as a good man to work for; and John was the salt of the earth. In Fat's book, a better man than John Hardin never lived.

There was a man by the name of Bill Purdy working for the Hardins and one named Wilson and a little old gnarled and knotty-muscled man by the name of Peck who was grub-spoiler for the outfit. A kid named Pink Forehand was a sort of cook's helper and general handy boy for the whole bunch.

This crew gathered the cattle and shaped up a mixed herd of seven hundred head and threw them on the cross-country trail to Ozona.

The days of the big history-making cow drives were over, of course, and had been for better than twenty years. Railroads and barbwire fences had changed all that by the turn of the century. But, in 1916, West Texas still had a lot of open country, so that a trail outfit, by driving across the big ranches and going around fenced farms and smaller ranches by way of lanes, could still make a three- or four-hundred-mile drive without an unreasonable amount of difficulty.

They started the drive in late November, and while the days were warm enough, the nights were plenty cold. Fat, who'd never been out much at night this time of the year, soon discovered that a tarp and a couple of quilts made a pretty skimpy bed. He'd lie on the hard ground and shake and shiver all night. John Hardin al-

3

ways claimed that the only reason his youngest cow-hand didn't freeze on that trip was that the vibrations of his snoring kept him warm with exercise.

Fat had ridden better horses than the ones the Hardins owned. As he told John, he could have gone to a thicket and cut himself a kid's stick-horse and been better mounted.

Then there was the grub. It was all right, as grub goes: red beans and potatoes. But when that menu of red beans and potatoes lasts week after week, with the only variation being potatoes and red beans, a man gets to where he'd like a change to pinto beans, at least.

However, Fat wasn't complaining. This still beat cotton picking. And he got along pretty well till the night of the stampede. This was Fat's first stampede, and the fact that he caused it didn't make it any less frightening.

They'd bedded down the herd on Kickapoo Creek, and John and Fat rolled out about three o'clock in the morning to ride guard till daylight. The night was black as the insides of a cow. A spitting rain was falling and freezing to their slickers as it hit. John was trying to sing to the bedded cattle, making him up a song as he went along. It wasn't much of a song to listen to, but cows don't seem to have much of an ear for notes, and Fat sure didn't; so that pretty well evened up things, all around.

Except for the fact that Fat's feet were getting so cold. He could feel his toes rattling around in his boots like marbles. He lifted his legs and crossed them in front of the saddle horn, getting them up under his

4

slicker, out of the wind. But this proved to be more solid comfort than he could stand.

He dozed off for a second. His horse moved, and out of the saddle Fat tumbled. The first thing that hit the ground was his head. And if he'd cut loose with a six-shooter, Fat couldn't have done a better job of stampeding the herd.

He came to, with the ground shaking under him. The cattle were already on their feet and quitting the country.

The stampede spooked Fat's horse. While Fat fought the animal, trying to get back into the saddle, he could hear the crashing and popping of the scrub mesquites breaking before the headlong rush of frantic cattle. From down at the wagon came the voice of Chris Hardin, crying out the warning that has brought many a sleeping cowhand up out of his bedroll with a sudden rush of fear.

"Roll out, boys! They're a-running!"

Fat got aboard again and spurred his horse in the direction the cattle had gone. He rode through a night so black he couldn't find his face with his hands. What he could do if he happened to catch the cattle, he didn't know. He couldn't see them. All he could do was imagine what would happen if his running horse tripped in a gulley or planted a foot in a prairie-dog hole.

The cattle ran pretty much in a body at first, and Fat, guided only by sound, managed to stay with them. Then, as the first wild rush of fear wore off, the cattle slowed and began to scatter. Fat would hear a little bunch pull off to the right, then another shift toward

5

the left. Finally, he could hear no more cattle running, just the heavy breathing and an occasional bawl of some lost and confused animal.

Fat attached himself to one of these smaller bunches. He rode around it, turned it back in the direction he thought the wagon was, and trailed along behind the grass-muffled sounds of their plodding hoofs.

He wished the cattle would stop; he ached from head to foot with the numbing cold. He wanted to get down and build a fire. But he stayed with his cattle till day broke and he began to hear other riders bringing little bunches of stragglers back toward the wagon. He knew then that he'd been right to stay with his bunch, that he was playing his part as a cowhand.

It was a cold and weary group of riders who finally pieced the scattered herd together back at the wagon a couple of hours after sunup. They strung the cattle out and trailed them past Chris Hardin and watched him tie a knot in a saddle string for each hundred head he counted. And when the last cow went past, Chris tied the seventh knot and nodded. They'd been luckier than most. They hadn't lost one head.

Riding toward the campfire, John Hardin, gray-faced with cold and fatigue, said to Fat, "Fat, what in the hell do you reckon happened to spook them cows?"

Fat wasn't about to admit to anything as ridiculous as going to sleep and falling out of his saddle.

"Mister Hardin," he said in sober innocence, "I just don't have no idea."

2

THE punishment Fat had taken on the drive down to Val Verde County merely whetted his appetite for more cow work. But before he could land another job, hard luck threw a wrench into his plans. A drouth had hit the country, the worst drouth in the history of Central Texas. The streams quit running; water holes dried up; wells failed; the leaves on century-old oaks and elms withered, then died. And around the dried-up water holes and wells gathered cattle so starved that their hides hung slack over their bone racks. Some of the cattle were able to mill and bawl. Some could only stand, weaving, while they gazed with great staring eyes out over the heat-blasted landscape. Some sank to the ground and lay quiet, watching with indifference while the air filled with wheeling buzzards, and the buzzards circled closer.

With cattle starving to death all over the country, there were no ranch jobs to be had. There weren't even any cotton-picking jobs, for that matter. And with World War I skyrocketing the price of food and clothing, Fat's father, Julius Alford, soon found himself unable to provide for his wife and several children.

It wasn't just a case of being short of money and having to skimp, a thing the family had been used to all their lives. It was now a matter of whether or not they ate. Something had to be done.

7

So they left the drouth-stricken area and moved to Victoria, in South Texas, where Fat went right back to the job he hated worst of any—cotton picking.

He picked cotton all that fall. He helped his father put in a cotton crop on rented land the following spring. Then, when excessive rains ruined that cotton crop, Fat went back to Coleman County and picked enough cotton to help get his folks back home on the farm near Valera.

That done, he was finished. He was seventeen now, and considered himself his own man. So he patched up his saddle gear, then did what many another youngster of his time and background had done before him—he saddled a horse and rode West. Out there, in some of that country he'd ridden through on the drive to Juno, there'd be a riding job of some sort, and he aimed to find it.

The day he left, he told his folks that if ever again they caught him humped up between two cotton rows, they'd know he'd gone stark raving mad.

"And the thing to do," he advised, "is to take a gun and shoot me between the eyes."

It was a man-size country for a job-hunting kid to wander out into. The trans-Pecos, some call it, which offhand means all that part of Texas west of the Pecos River. But that doesn't get it all. Because some of the same sort of country and the same sort of people are on the east side of the river. The only real boundary to the region is the Rio Grande, looping far south in its big bend to get around the Chisos Mountains. Everything south of the Rio Grande is Mexico; but the boundaries

8

of the rest of the trans-Pecos country have more than anything else to do with how a man lives and how wide is his imagination.

It's a fantastic country. High, bald ridges. Wide mesquite flats. Crawling desert sands. Gushing springs, some hot, some cold. Salt lakes. Grassy swags. Greasewood slopes. Flat-topped mesas. Deep tortuous canyons. Great desert plains sweeping up to pine-studded mountains, and the mountains standing blue in the distance.

It's a country of drouths and floods, of bitter cold winds and dry, searing heat, of mirages and "devil witch" whirlwinds, of coyotes and antelope and blue quail, of oil derricks standing thick as forests in the greasewood flats, and walking-johnny pumps sucking black stinking fortunes from the bowels of the earth, of cactus and sotol and soapweed and ocotillo, of little kangaroo rats that balance on tails longer than their bodies.

It's a country of cattle, horses, sheep, and goats, counted by the hundreds of thousands. It's a country where a rancher doesn't measure his holdings by the acre—he owns it by sections, six hundred and forty acres to the section. It's a country where men can recollect when they drove the Mexicans and Indians from the land, then turned on each other and fought like starved wolves for possession of it, and finally turned "respectable" and called on the Law to help them hold it from the plundering thieves who tried to grab it from them.

Some claim it's the richest land on the face of the earth, and some claim it's the poorest, the difference of opinion hinging mainly on who got there first and how much land he was able to take and hold.

All that, Fat was to learn later. Right then, he was just a shirttail kid on the lookout for a horseback job to get him out of the cotton patch, and this looked like the sort of country where it might be found.

3

THERE was this man by the name of Mack Adams. He was wagon boss for the Elsinore Cattle Company operating in the alkali country out of Fort Stockton.

Some cowhands didn't like to work for Adams. They said that when you signed on under him, you might just as well swap off your bedroll for a lantern, because you weren't going to sleep anyhow.

But when Adams died, there were some good things that could be said about him. Like the fact that he'd hire a strange kid without any recommendations or cowboy experience to speak of and give him a chance to make a hand.

That's what Adams did for Fat, and Fat has never forgotten. About the only fault Fat ever found with his boss was Adams' aversion to a rider's practicing with a rope.

Adams set Fat straight on that the first day. He told his new rider that he didn't hold with having the E L cattle roped and jerked around any more than had to be, and that the thing for Fat to do was keep his rope on his saddle till he needed it.

Which sounded sort of foolish to Fat. He couldn't see how Adams expected him to be ready to rope a cow when he needed to if he couldn't keep in practice. But he didn't argue. He was just a kid, new to the job,

11

and he wanted to hold it. He kept his rope on the saddle—till a day came when the temptation was too great.

Adams was fixing to ship a little handful of stuff, three carloads of steers that were fat and ready for market. The crew set out early one morning on the two-day drive for the shipping pens. Adams sent Fat on ahead with the *remuda*, the extra cow horses, telling him to hold them at Wild Horse Water Hole, where the crew would noon. The hands would ride the extra horses that afternoon.

Fat couldn't have liked the job better if he'd picked it. He jogged along, admiring how the grass lay green on the wide rolling prairies and how the sunlight flashed on the tossing manes and tails of the loose horses romping ahead. He could sing a little if he felt like it, or put in his time trying to roll a Bull Durham cigarette.

All the grown cowhands smoked; Fat figured maybe he ought to take up the habit.

But jogging along in the saddle didn't prove to be the best place to learn to roll cigarettes. After wasting considerable tobacco, Fat tucked his sack back in his pocket and speeded up his ride with a shout and a wave of his hat at the horses. He could see he wouldn't get a smoke till he could get his feet flat on the ground.

The loose horses were frisky and about half hunting an excuse to run. They broke into a gallop and made it to the water hole in about a third of the time they would have normally taken. Fat wasn't too concerned with the fact that they weren't near as fresh for riding any more as they might have been.

12

The Wild Horse Water Hole lay in a shallow draw, and just above it was plenty of good grazing. Fat watered the horses and turned them out on the grass, knowing they'd stay close, then led his horse to the shade of a mesquite. There, he squatted to practice rolling cigarettes again.

But even there on the ground, he found he wasn't too good. Try as he might, the best sort of a quirley he could twist up looked more like a fat worm in a cocoon than a cigarette. And when he tried to light it, he singed his eyebrows with the lighted match and didn't get but a couple of puffs from his cigarette before all the tobacco grains spilled out, leaving him to suck on the empty paper.

Fat spat the paper out in disgust and sat staring vacantly into space with a vague feeling of frustration, wondering what to get at next.

Into the line of his vision moved a muley cow that had grazed down to water and was now getting a drink. Fat looked at her speculatively. She was a big heavy sister, all right—and there was that hard-twist rope of his on his saddle. That rope was brand-new and had never been on anything heavy enough to pull the stretch out of it.

The muley wore the E L brand; still Adams was back yonder, trailing along with the slow-traveling steers. He wouldn't be coming in here for another couple of hours. There'd be no reason for him to know about it if a man was to run the cow off before Adams arrived.

Fat got up and tightened the cinch on his horse, then climbed into the saddle. He ran out a loop in his rope. The horse was a good one; he had already for-

13

gotten more about cow work than Fat knew. So when Fat headed him toward the muley and cut him down the side of one hind leg with his loop, the horse got right down to business. He put Fat up within roping distance before the muley was aware they were after her.

Fat whirled his loop a couple of times and let fly. At the same instant that his loop encircled the cow's head, Fat's horse threw himself into a squat that planted both forefeet apart and set the root of his tail against the ground.

Braced like that, the way a good roping horse should be, he couldn't have been budged by anything smaller than a runaway train. But with the big heavy muley running as fast as she was, straight away from them, something had to give.

What gave was Fat's rope. It was a new one and built for heavy roping, but in this case the roping was too heavy. It snapped in the middle. Fat's end of it came flying back at him, rolling up into a wad about the size of a hat just before it slammed against his forehead with a force that came close to blinding him.

Blood flew in all directions. Fat reeled in his saddle. He slid to the ground, where he knelt with his hands clasped to his bleeding face. He was done dead and he knew it. Nobody could bleed and hurt like he was without dying. He moaned and groaned, waiting for death, hoping it'd come in a hurry.

But death seemed slow in coming, and Fat's misery kept getting worse. Finally, he lost patience and wiped enough blood out of his eyes to find his way to the

14

water hole. There he lay down and washed his face in the cool water.

He felt better after that and thought maybe he might live if he could get the bleeding stopped. He washed and washed, but still the blood kept trickling down his face and spattering his shirt and leggings. Before long, he was as bloody as a fresh beef. At last, he removed his shirt and washed it and hung it over a bush to dry; and while he was busy at that, the drying wind got a chance at his face and congealed the blood, so that it quit oozing.

Before long, Fat heard the sound of the chuckwagon topping a rise not far from the water hole. He grabbed up his half-dry shirt and started putting it on while his mind jumped around like a frog trapped in a bucket, trying to figure out what sort of excuse to make. He knew the steer drive and Adams wouldn't be far behind that wagon, and, in the pitiful-looking shape he was in now, he'd better have the answers for questions somebody was sure to ask him.

He mounted and rode toward the horse herd to give himself time to think. After he'd thought awhile, he hitched the rest of his rope to a small scraggly half-green mesquite and had his horse uproot it. He rode off, dragging the mesquite to the water hole, where already the Mexican cook had stopped the chuckwagon and was starting dinner. The Mexican took one look at Fat's face and wanted to know what was the matter. Fat told him he'd gone out to drag up some wood for a dinner fire and had broken his rope against a tree he was trying to pull down, and look what it had done to his face!

15

The Mexican didn't appear to swallow that yarn, but he didn't say anything. Fat left his wood and rode back toward the horses. He wished he'd thought up a better lie, but knew he was stuck with this one, now that he'd told it.

The cook got dinner, and here came the rest of the cowhands, with the bawling steers streaming down to water. Part of the riders kept a loose herd on the steers while the others ate; then they swapped about.

By now, in spite of all his hurting, Fat was hungry enough to gnaw wood. But he wasn't about to ride down there and try to make his story stick with all those cowhands who knew how itchy his roping hand was. He made a big show of keeping a close watch on the horse herd, although the horses didn't have any notion of leaving such good grazing grounds. When a rider finished eating and motioned for a new mount, Fat would cut out a horse and start it in a run toward camp for the man to rope. But Fat never ventured close enough for anybody to get a good look at his face.

After a while, the rest of the crew started the steers away from water and on toward town. Fat figured they'd all left the wagon, and if he'd hurry he might get a bite or two before the cook broke camp. He rode toward the wagon in a gallop and had already dismounted before he saw Seth Fry rise up from the far side of the wagon, where he'd been patching some of his gear. And then, it had to be Fat's luck that the boss Adams came riding back about this time.

Adams said, "Goshamighty, boy! What in the world happened to you?"

Fat told his little tree-pulling story all over again,

16

just like he'd explained it to the Mexican cook. About the time he finished, he glanced at Seth Fry. That cowhand was looking out from under the brim of his hat at Fat and licking sun-cracked lips to hide a knowing grin. Which made Fat more aware than ever of how thin his story must sound and how close he was to getting fired for roping a cow just for practice.

But Adams didn't seem to suspect a thing. He expressed a lot of concern for how badly Fat was hurt and offered to take him to a doctor. But Fat said no, that he was doing just fine, that there was no use in wasting time and money on a doctor, and he went to rummaging in the chuckbox for something to eat.

Pulling the wool over Adams' eyes like he'd done made Fat feel pretty smart and keen-witted. And that night, when they'd bedded down the steers and pitched camp, he made another try at rolling a cigarette and came out with one as smooth as any ready-roll a smoker ever hung a lip over. Fat made certain that all the hands got a good look at that cigarette when he lit up.

That's when the cowhands started in on him. First they made sure that Adams was close enough to hear, then Fry called on Fat to tell all over again how he'd gotten hurt. One of the other boys said that was the dangedest thing he'd ever heard of and asked Fat how come the rope hit him in the face, instead of the back of his head. Fat told him he'd been looking right down the rope when it broke. Then another one wanted to know how Fat could have been looking down the rope if he'd been pulling against the tree. Fat thought for a minute, then said he'd been looking back over his

17

shoulder. And one would quiz him on one point of his story and another on some other point, all the time looking sly grins at one another and glancing up at Adams to see if he was catching on.

Finally Adams told them all to shut up and go to bed, that they didn't have any more reason to doubt Fat's word than Fat had to lie about getting hurt.

It wasn't till years later that Adams admitted to Fat that he'd seen the muley cow wearing Fat's loop around her neck before he'd ever ridden up to the water hole that day.

4

I N those days, the Elsinore was about an average-size ranch for West Texas. The owners had around five hundred sections of land under control. In good years, when the rains fell right and the grama grass stood tall and green as a wheat field, the outfit ran around fifteen thousand head of cattle. A part of this herd were big three- and four-year-old steers, but most of it was she-stuff, grazed for the calf crop they'd produce.

The herds browsed over the same range the year round, and nobody ever thought of winterfeeding. That was back when the grass was still so good that winterfeeding wasn't necessary.

The cows started dropping calves in March, and generally the wagon for the spring roundup rolled about the first of April. Unless, of course, the big steers were to be sent to the blue-grass country of Oklahoma and Kansas for priming. Then the spring roundup started early enough to get the steer gather out of the way before the calf work started.

The wagon boss was in charge of the roundup. With a crew of some fifteen cowhands, he would generally wind up the spring work on the Elsinore in about three months. During the summer, ranch work slacked off, with nothing much for the hands to do except hunt and doctor "wormies," and make certain the windmills were producing water. Then, around the first of September, the fall roundup began, when the calves, now weighing some four hundred pounds, were gathered and trailed to the nearest shipping point and sent to market.

Of it all, Fat liked the spring roundup best. He liked the coming of warm weather after a long winter of blizzards. He liked to see the green tips of the young grass pushing up through the gray of the winter-dead turf. He liked the fun and excitement of working out in the open with a crew of young bloods who lived free and easy and were inclined to damn the consequences of most any act they took a notion to perform. He liked to lie out under the stars of a night and listen to one coyote making enough yap for a dozen and watch a spring moon climb high, bathing the rolling prairies with its pale light.

The day's work began early. Around four o'clock in the morning, the cook built up the campfire and started rattling pots and pans as he dragged them from the chuckbox. This was the signal for the horse wrangler to roll out, saddle his night horse, and ride in search of the grazing *remuda*.

The cowhands had it easy. They didn't stir till the coffee started boiling, sending out its tantalizing aroma. Then out they'd come, and that's when the swearing started.

Some of the swearing might be on account of stiff, sore muscles from the previous day's work. Most of it, however, had to do with tight-fitting boots that wouldn't slip on over dew-damp socks. It is well worth a man's time to study the sight of several half-dressed cowhands bent over to hang to their bootstraps while

20

they crow-hop around their bedrolls on one bare foot. The swearing is as colorful and original as men living free of women can make it, and Fat claims the only thing he ever heard to beat it was the praying that one cowhand did every morning—calling for divine help to get his boot on.

They dressed—in boots with heels high enough to keep a man's foot from running through a stirrup; spurs heavy enough to knock the fight out of a bad horse in a hurry and help a man keep his balance on him; Levi britches because they're tough; bullhide batwing chaps to shed brush and rain and cold; neckerchiefs to keep the sun off a man's neck; and in wide-brimmed hats that'll shed sun and rain, fan a branding fire, dip water, or whip a fighting cow in the face.

The cowhand's next move was to tie up his bedroll and pitch it on the ground beside the wagon. Failure to perform this little chore was just asking the camp cook to leave it when he moved the wagon later on.

If it was a shivery-cold morning, the cook would allow a rider to pour himself a cup of coffee before breakfast was ready—but only if the man backed off away from the fire to squat and drink it. Cow camp cooks were notoriously cranky individuals, and the greenhorn who didn't have sense enough to keep out of the cook's way while he prepared a meal soon got set straight on that matter.

Breakfast generally consisted of beefsteak and sour-dough biscuits baked in a Dutch oven, with a little black molasses thrown in for sweetening. Sometimes there'd be oatmeal, but no milk for it. Who ever heard of milk in a cow camp?

21

About the time the crew was sopping the last of the molasses out of their tin plates, here'd come the wrangler, bringing in the *remuda* at a gallop. A man might not be quite through eating, but it didn't matter. Right then, it was time to pitch his eating tools into the washtub set out for that purpose, and grab himself a rope.

The wrangler needed a place to corral his horses, and that corral had to be built in a hurry—out of men and ropes. It was built on the order of a kid's merry-go-round, the main difference being that there were some thirty feet of rope held between each of the men, and the circle wasn't closed till the horses had been run through the gap.

Into this corral would come the stamping, snorting *remuda,* each horse crowding and kicking, looking for an escape hole but seldom finding it before the corral was drawn shut behind him.

The wagon boss did the roping. There were fifteen men, each with his special string of ten horses and each calling for the particular mount he'd ride that day. One would call for old "Peewee," another for "Cannon Ball." There'd be "Hell's Angel," and "Redbird," and "Liverpill," and "Screwtail," and "Stump Sucker," and "Pearly Gates," and "Leaping Lena," and "Darling Jill." A hundred and fifty, maybe two hundred head of horses. And yet, with day just barely breaking and no real light to see by, the wagon boss recognized each horse called for, reached into the milling herd with his loop and brought it out—and was embarrassed as all hell on those rare occasions when he made a mistake.

With the horses caught, the saddling and mounting

started, and with it started the fun. Always, even in the best sort of *remuda*, there'd be a good number of horses still determined not to pack men on their backs. Trying to change those horses' minds quite often resulted in rough and unexpected doings.

By the time this early-morning show was over, every cowhand in the crew was wide awake and ready for work; so the boss led them out for a swing drive over country they hadn't worked the day before. He'd drop one man off here and one a little further along till the last man, riding the outside swing, had such a big circle to cover that he sometimes had to hunt and drive cattle at a gallop in order to reach the designated water hole or holding ground by the time the rest got there.

They'd pull in to the holding grounds around dinner-time or a little past, each man driving before him his morning gather of bawling cows and calves. They'd throw the cattle together, around three hundred head, and the cattle would mill and bawl and churn up dust with their hoofs.

The cook, who'd already moved his four-mule wagon to this new camp site, would start beating on a dishpan with an iron spoon.

"Come an' git it!" he'd bawl out, touching off an immediate horse race from the holding grounds to camp, with every man spurring for the first plate of beans. Three or four unlucky ones were left to hold the herd bunched till the others had eaten.

There was no time for rest at noon. A man ate, swapped his saddle to the back of a fresh horse, and rode out to the herd to start the real work of the day.

Branding fires were started and fanned till the blaze

23

heated the running irons to glowing cherry red. The ropers went to work—generally two of them—catching calves out of the herd, heeling the biggest ones, catching the little ones around the neck. The ropers dragged their catches toward the branding fires, and the flankers fell on them, wrestling them to the ground.

When everything came off right, a flanker could get hold of a calf, reach across his back, grab a handhold in his flank, give a yank as the calf jumped, roll him in the air, and bust him against the ground hard enough that the calf would lie there till the flanker could get on him, using his weight to hold the calf down.

But when something slipped, and it quite often did, then it was sometimes a hard matter to figure out which one was throwing which. Calf and man would get locked up, leg in arm, and around and around they'd go, with the calf bawling and the man swearing, and the iron man trying to fight them away from his branding fire.

Every cowhand knows that a calf is born with only four feet. But there are flankers who'll take a solemn cowhand oath that the minute you start to throw some calves, the animals sprout eight or ten extras. They claim that nothing with only four feet could kick so hard and so fast and from so many different directions at once.

So many flankers have lost front teeth before this whirlwind of flailing hoofs that a gapped mouth has become a sort of trademark of the cowhand profession. In fact, some riders claim that a full set of front teeth is a distinct handicap in getting work at a new place. The wagon boss figures that a cowhand who's never had a tooth kicked out of his head is either short of experience or is a deadhead who won't step in and really take hold of a job.

When finally the calf was stretched out, here came one man with a branding iron and another with a knife. And what those two did to the calf in the next couple of minutes proved to the calf that he ought to have fought harder. When finally released to go in search of his mother, the calf had been marked, dehorned, branded, and castrated.

The knife man generally kept a sack handy, into which he tossed the bloody cods he'd removed from the bull calves. These were termed "mountain oysters," and were to be fried for supper.

Among the cowhands Fat worked with, it was a common belief that the consumption of "mountain oysters" greatly increased a man's potency, and any time one expected to do some heavy courting, he made a point of eating plenty of them.

Throughout the afternoon, the work went on, hot and heavy. The churned-up dust fogged thicker and higher above the bawling clamor, carrying with it the mingled odors of horse sweat, man sweat, blood, wood smoke, and scorched hair.

Sometimes the heavy work grew monotonous; but generally, before that happened, a rider would let an angry cow charge between the holdup men. A flanker or iron man would glance up, and there that old mad sister would be, coming right at him with her horns drooped and blood in her eye. The man would let out a yell and whip her in the face with his hat till he could get to his feet; then he'd make a fast run for cover.

25

He'd duck around the first horse he came to and let the cow go by, then come back, swearing at all the whooping and jeering cowhands who had stopped to watch the show. Sometimes he'd get mad and offer to fist-whip the holdup man who'd allowed the cow to charge him; but usually he let it go. At least, the incident had put a little variety into the afternoon's work.

Finally, along about sundown, a roper waved a hand as a signal that the last calf had been through the mill. Then the riders holding the herd rode away from it, giving the cattle a chance to scatter. The lost calves located their mothers, who sniffed at the burned and bloody wounds of their offspring and lifted their heads to bawl in outraged protest.

For the men, it was strip the gear from tired and sweaty horses, wash up, eat a leisurely supper, swap a few lies about their experiences with bad horses, good liquor, and reluctant women, then heave their hotrolls from the wagon and bed down for the night.

Some might stay up an hour later, playing poker on a saddle blanket spread out in the campfire light, but these games seldom amounted to much. Money was scarce, the men bone-tired, and, by daylight next morning, they'd be back in the saddle, riding out to comb a new part of the range.

5

SINCE ranch work is seasonal, a rancher needs as many men as he can afford to hire during the roundup. The rest of the time, he has no use for the extra hands. During the summer and winter periods, he keeps a skeleton crew and lets the others go until he needs to round up again.

When the work played out on the Elsinore, Fat rode away from it and was glad to go. There'd been nothing wrong with the job; but out in the Davis Mountains and down in the Big Bend and across the Rio Grande into Mexico was a lot of wild new country he wanted to see.

A couple of days after leaving the ranch, he met a rider out in the middle of a greasewood flat.

The stranger pulled up and said, "Howdy."

Fat did the same.

The stranger wanted to know if Fat was looking for a job and Fat said he was and the stranger asked, "Well, what can you do?"

"What have you got?" Fat wanted to know.

The man said that he had a couple of horses that needed breaking.

Fat said that was just his dish, intimating that he was an old horsebreaker from 'way back yonder.

The man studied the squat young rider for a while, like maybe he doubted him, but finally told him to

27

come on. So they rode through the greasewood in a fog of alkali dust churned up by their horses' hoofs, and after a while they came to a ranch house, where the man led Fat out to the corrals to show him the horses.

They were handsome young animals, all right, a bay and a brown. Fat saw that they'd make the man a pair of good mounts, once they were broken to ride. But, from the rope marks on them and the way they hit for the far side of the pen the minute he rode up, Fat figured that some horsebreaker had already taken a whack at these ponies and hadn't done a very cute job. They'd been messed with just enough to make them hard to manage.

The horses were still backed up against the far side of the pen, snorting, when the man's wife left the house and came out, to start telling Fat how the horses ought to be handled. She was a big woman, with a big voice, and it was plain to Fat from the start who wore the britches in this family. Fat treated her mighty respectful, saying, "Yes, ma'am," and "No, ma'am," as he dismounted and went about unsaddling his own horse.

Fat thought that if he could keep quiet long enough for her to talk herself out, maybe she'd go on back to the house, where she belonged. So he took his time about stripping the gear off his horse, then led it to a watering trough and finally let the animal take a good roll in the dust before tying him up.

But the delay was wasted. Sister Big Britches hadn't the least notion of going back to the house. She was still right there beside him, telling him how to break horses, when Fat finally took his rope off the saddle and ran out a loop.

The young broncs watched Fat come through the gate. They bannered their tails and stomped their forefeet against the ground; they threw up their heads and started whistling, like Fat was a panther that had them cornered. Whoever had made the first try at breaking them had done one thing: he'd sure made them warlike.

Suddenly the bay backed his ears and came straight at Fat, all set to run him down. Fat stood with his loop cocked till the horse got close, then stepped aside and picked up the bronc's forefeet. Throwing his weight back against the rope, he turned the running outlaw heels over head.

Big Britches went to tromping on one foot and then the other. "I told you not to do that," she raved at Fat. "I told you I wouldn't put up with having my horses mistreated. I told you that it was rough handling that spoiled them. If you'd treat them gentle, like I said, you'd have no trouble!"

Fat waited for the stunned horse to get to his feet, then led it to one end of the pen. There, the man held the rope while Fat went up it, hand over hand, till he could get hold of the horse's ears. The bay tried to paw him, but Fat managed to keep his ear-hold and stay away from those chopping hoofs till the man could bring a hackamore and slip it over the bronc's head. Then Fat tied the horse to a post and made another loop in his rope.

Big Britches still had both ends of her tongue going as Fat stepped toward the second bronc.

The brown made for Fat just like the bay had, his hoofs hammering the corral hardpan.

"Now, you be careful with this one," Big Britches

29

yelled at him; and Fat nodded and said, "Yes, ma'am," and picked up the brown's forefeet and let him to the ground harder than he had the first.

Sister Big Britches was all but foaming at the mouth by the time Fat and her husband had tied this bronc to a corral post.

The brown was frantic. He lunged against the rope, bawling his rage. He reared up and tried to climb out. Failing that, he fell back and lay on the ground and began hammering his head against the fence poles.

"Turn him loose!" the woman shouted. "Turn him loose before he kills himself."

"He'll quit," Fat said, "when his head gets sore enough."

Suddenly Big Britches shrieked at him, "Young man, I'll give you just fifteen minutes to turn that horse loose and get off this ranch!"

Fat reached for his hat, raised it, and bowed low. "Ma'am," he said gallantly, "I'll give you ten minutes of that time back. And you can turn the horse loose yourself."

Fat had ridden about a quarter of a mile down the road when he finally twisted around in his saddle for a farewell look. Best he could tell, the bronc was still beating his head against the fence, Big Britches was still going around in circles, and the old man was standing off to one side, looking sort of forlorn.

The distance being what it was by now, Fat never was real sure; but he thought the old man waved at him just before he went out of sight around a point of a low ridge.

6

MOST young cowhands take pride in their independence, and Fat was no exception. The way he tipped his hat and rode away from a horsebreaking job he'd held for less than an hour was a fair indication of the pattern he was to follow for the rest of his cowhand days, the pattern that most working cowhands followed.

He tipped his hat to Sister Big Britches and rode off to take a job with Lon Slaughter, who operated a cow outfit along the Pecos River. From there, he drifted out to the W. S. Warren ranch in the Big Bend and then to the 7N outfit belonging to the Hendersons, and then on to so many different jobs at so many different places that he can no longer recollect happenings in their proper sequence. He admits that might not have been the smartest way to work, but that's how he did it and how he came by a wide variety of cowhand adventures that make for good recollections—recollections which today he "wouldn't take a purty for."

But, as he was soon to learn, drifting from job to job has its disadvantages; the main one being the sort of mounts a drifter draws.

The regular hands of a cow outfit always have the best horses in the *remuda* spotted; what the newcomer gets is the leavings. And the best that can be said of such mounts is that they keep the work from getting monotonous.

Generally, they're horses that have been spoiled by some horsebreaker who didn't know his business. Or sometimes they've been ridden only four or five saddles before the ranch owner decides they're "broke enough for a cowhand to make out on." Which means they can be saddled and mounted; from there on, it's just up to the rider to do enough work on them to earn his wages.

Lon Slaughter hired Fat to help with a gather of sixteen hundred head of fat calves he was sending to market. When Fat rode out to the wagon camp at the Girvin shipping pens on the Pecos, he found the crew short of horses.

A cow horse under the saddle of a hard-working cowhand takes a lot of punishment in a very short time. If each rider doesn't have eight or ten horses to draw from, he's soon "afoot."

The crew boss climbed up and sat on the hind wheel of the chuckwagon to consider the problem. Finally, he said, "Boys, Fat, here, has got to have some horses to ride, and all I can see to do is for each of us to cut him one out of our strings. That'll leave us only five apiece, so we'll have to take mighty good care of them till the roundup's done."

Fat watched a smile broaden the mouth of a cowhand by the name of Son Lawhon. "Why," Son said generously, "I've got an old horse that I'd be proud for Fat to ride."

"Now, ain't that a fact?" Bucky Canlon put in. "You take that old brown horse I drawed. Ain't another cow horse on the Pecos like him!"

When Fat mounted Son's horse, he saw why that cowhand had been so generous. Twice the horse reared straight up on his hind legs and came over backwards. Each time Fat managed to step off quick enough to keep from being crushed against the earth. When the horse tried it the third time, Fat laid the butt end of his quirt between the outlaw's ears, striking him harder than he aimed to. The horse dropped like he'd been shot. But it didn't kill him, and after he'd lain there awhile, beating his head against the ground and bawling, he finally came to his feet. Fat mounted him and they went on about the day's work.

But Bucky Canlon's brown was a real surprise to Fat. The first time Fat roped him out of the *remuda,* the horse fell back against the rope, fighting it with his forefeet the way many horses do. But then Brown changed tactics. He came straight at Fat, breasting into him and knocking him flat; then he moved up to stand over him, snorting and stomping.

Fat rolled clear. Brown let him get nearly to his feet, then knocked him down again. Fat got to his hands and knees, and Brown struck him down with a leg. Fat tried to crawl away, and it was the same thing. Any way he went, Brown was right there, standing over him, stomping the ground with heavy hoofs that could easily pound the life out of Fat.

Finally, Fat gave up and lay where he was. He looked toward the other cowhands and saw them all bent over with laughter. Fat guessed there was some sort of joke to the predicament he was in, but he'd just be damned if he saw it.

"I'd sure appreciate it," he said finally, "if some of you laughing idjits would come get this horse off me."

Son Lawhon came over and backed the horse away from Fat. "Old Brown's been whip-broke," he said, by way of explanation.

Fat got up off the ground and dusted himself. "Yeah," he said, not knowing what Son meant by whip-broke, but not wanting to show his ignorance.

"Yeah," Son said. "The man that broke him would rope him and then whip him with a blacksnake if he didn't walk right up to him. Old Brown was just afraid you was coming at him with a whip, so he came at you first. If you'd just put your hands on him, instead of trying to dodge, he'd a-knowed you wasn't going to whip him and would a-stood still. Old Brown's a real pet."

Every *remuda* has its quota of runaways, and some of them, once they get started, act like they've gone crazy. They'll run head on into a tree, jump off a cliff, or tear out in a dead run through rocks and boulders. Sooner or later, they're bound to fall and break a leg or hurt a rider.

Lewis Yates used a method for stopping these runaways that worked pretty well. Lewis was one of the Yates brothers who operated a cow outfit out on the Pecos. Fat rode for them some, back in the days before the Yates boys struck it rich in oil and Lewis still worked cattle, right along with the hands he hired.

They were out with the chuckwagon, and one morning Lewis saddled a big rawboned horse that broke into a wild run the minute he felt Lewis' weight on his back.

Fat was fighting his own horse at the moment, but got him under control in time to look up and see Lewis and his outlaw go down in a boil of alkali dust about a hundred yards off. Fat rode toward them, afraid Lewis was hurt. Before he got there, out of the dust fog charged the horse, with Lewis still aboard.

Then down they went again in another wild scramble of hoofs and dust.

Fat got to them this time as they came to their feet. He said to Lewis, "What're you doing? Throwing that horse?"

"Sure am," Lewis said. "And I'll keep throwing the old fool till I break him from running."

Fat wanted to know how, and Lewis told him to follow along and watch.

Lewis let the runaway get going good, then yanked the horse's head around to the left side. At the same time, Lewis bent his left knee and shoved it hard against the horse's shoulder.

Down went the runaway, to turn a complete wildcat. But Lewis' weight was on the top side, and all he had to do was step off before the horse hit the ground.

"It don't take many falls like that," Lewis said, "to get one educated out of that running."

It looked to Fat like a mighty neat trick if a man's nerve and timing were good. But he could see that if a rider had to pull it on rocky or gullied ground, he stood a good chance of breaking his horse's neck. And maybe his own.

Fat discovered a rather unique way of stopping a runaway. He and Walter Capps were cow hunting in Bee Canyon south of Ozona, where the rocks and sotol and cedars stood so thick and tall a man couldn't see anywhere except straight up. Fat was riding high up, next to the rim, when he jumped a cow. She took off down the slant with her tail in the air and her hocks a-rattling, and Fat hooked spurs to his horse and went after her.

The brush was popping and the rocks were flying. Fat was mounted on a fool horse that took the cold-jaw and couldn't be turned or stopped. He kept hauling back on the reins till finally the bits came apart in the horse's mouth. The bridle slipped back over the runaway's head and down on his neck. And here they went, at a pace that set Fat's scalp to crawling under his hat.

Fat wanted to step off but was afraid to on account of the rough ground. Yet he was just as afraid not to, because if that fool horse ever stumbled and lost his footing, the chances were Walter Capps would have to bring a hoe to scrape up what was left of him and the horse.

About that time, they caught up with the running cow, and Fat reached out with a big loop and laid it on. Right in front of them was a tall stand of cedars. The cow went around them on one side, while the horse took to the other. They all met on the far side, where the rope around those springy cedars piled the three of them in a heap on the ground.

While they were still scrambling to their feet, Walter Capps rode up and looked the situation over.

"Well," he said, "that's one way to stop them old runaways."

36

"Yeah," Fat said sourly, "but it's not one I'd recommend to just anybody."

For ornery bullheaded stubbornness in cow horses, Fat reckons a balker that belonged to the Bassetts, out in the Dryden country, beats anything he ever came across.

He was a big bay horse. Fat drew him on a roundup the Bassetts were making of some Mexico cattle they had on the graze. These cattle were wild as snakes in tall grass and could run like deer. If a man didn't have a real cow horse between his legs, he couldn't get within good hollering distance of them.

But mounted on this bay, Fat got along fine. The bay knew his business and was willing to do his work—until he got hot and mad. Then he was done. Right then he'd quit, and that's all there was to it.

Fat learned about this on a day when he'd ridden the bay extra hard after a work mule that had escaped an old man who was camped beside the Pecos River. The old man couldn't move his wagon till he'd caught the mule, and he couldn't catch the mule because the animal had taken up with a little band of wild mares running loose along the river.

When Fat learned of the old man's predicament, he offered to catch the mule for him and found it to be a bigger job than he'd anticipated. He located the mares and mule among a range of low hills not far from the river. The hill slopes were cut with a lot of deep gullies, and it seemed to make the big bay angry to have to jump these gullies with a rider on his back. Fat had to work him over a little with his spurs to push him up

37

within roping distance of the mule, and this made the bay madder still.

He was running with his ears back and his teeth bared when they plunged down into a deep wash, too wide to jump, and Fat reached out and laid the loop around the head of the mule scrambling up a still steeper slope on the opposite side.

And then, instead of squatting to take the load, the bay wheeled suddenly and took off down the draw, running wild. As a result, they just picked the mule right off the high bank and pulled him over backwards in the air.

Fat looked up in time to see the mule coming down square on top of him and knew he was a gone duck. But he'd reckoned without the speed of his horse. That hot and mad bay flat outran the pull of gravity on the high-flying mule, so that it hit the ground just behind them.

The mule landed on its back, with all four feet in the air, and that's the position he was still in after he'd been dragged fifty yards down the draw, where Fat finally got the bay pulled to a stop.

It was a pretty skinned-up mule that Fat delivered to the old man at the river, but the man seemed grateful to have him back, and Fat rode the sweating bay back down to the river to the shipping trap. There, the boss called on him to rope some calves out of the gather and drag them up to the branding fire.

And that's where the bay quit on him. Fat had picked up the heels of a calf and had dragged the bawling animal about halfway from the milling herd to the branding fire when the bay stopped.

Fat touched him with a spur. Nothing happened. He

38

spurred again and swore at the horse. The animal still stood. Fat went to work on him with a quirt, but it was wasted effort. That mule chase had gotten the bay hot and mad, and now he'd quit.

Other riders came to help Fat. The bay had balked right in the way of other ropers dragging heeled calves up to the fire. The men tried to move him by roping and dragging him. They nearly pulled his head off, but there wasn't another horse in the outfit strong enough to untrack him. The men whipped him from head to heels, using quirts and ropes and cow whips. The lashes made him flinch and tremble, finally made him squat and urinate. But when the men had worn themselves out, he was still right where he'd stopped, standing in his same tracks.

Fat doesn't try to excuse what the cowhands did to the bay later on in the day. Along about sundown, one of the crew came in from town with several bottles of tequila.

The riders were all squatted around the campfire, getting acquainted with the tequila while they waited for supper. And out there, where he'd stood all afternoon, was the balky bay, still holding down his same tracks. After the bottles had made a few rounds, some of the boys got to wondering just what would move that old horse.

Merle Hooper offered to bet that if he'd rope and jerk the bay down a couple of times, that'd change his mind about moving. He mounted and roped the bay's head and flipped the slack of his rope back of the bay's heels and made a run on it. The bay went down. But when Merle let him up, he stood set again. Merle tried it a second and third time. But when he finally took his rope off, the bay was standing in his original tracks.

Then somebody else took a drink and suggested branding the bay, saying he'd bet a hot iron would move the balky devil. So they heated a Block Y iron a cherry red and slapped it to his hip and held it. The smoke curled thick and yellow, and the scent of scorching hair and flesh grew hot in their nostrils. But when they pulled the iron away, the bay hadn't moved.

After that, they admitted complete defeat and went back to the tequila. The bay was still holding down his tracks when the bottles went dry and they all spread out their blankets on the sand and lay down for the night.

Some of the riders figured he'd still be standing there at daylight, but they were wrong. During the night some time, the bay evidently decided he'd won his point; the next morning, they found him grazing with the rest of the *remuda*.

Fat said he guessed he wasn't the only one ashamed of how they treated that old horse; he noticed the next time the bay balked nobody whipped him or swore at him. In fact, the riders seemed sort of respectful when they stripped the saddle off the balker and left him to stand till his mad wore off.

7

THE storybook cowhand is a noble creature, so chockful of principles and morals that the sight of a woman a hundred yards off will make him blush. The cowhand of fact is a young, vigorous, and lusty animal, who may or may not be shy around women, just owing to how much experience he's had, but who definitely understands what women are for. A job may hold him for months on some ranch, clear to the back side of nowhere and completely away from the sight and companionship of any woman; but, sooner or later, the urge for romance sends the blood coursing hot through his veins. Then, job or no job, he's a long time gone.

Fat and a couple of other cocky young cowhands were riding for the Kokernut outfit, out of Alpine. We'll call these boys Mac and Bunion. That isn't their names, but they're older now, no longer so hot-blooded, and what their wives and families don't know about their past may keep everybody a lot happier.

Came payday and a layoff. There were the three of them, with cash in their pockets and the green sap running high. Where to go? What to do?

Mac said, "How's about El Paso?"

El Paso was only a couple of hundred miles off. Mac had him a new sport-model car, a big swank sky-blue job, with wire wheels and a grandma seat in the back. Let the top down, and that automobile was a stunner

41

to any young female who got the horn blown at her. El Paso sounded like the right place.

The boys hit Alpine and the barbershop. They got haircuts and shaves. What grew on their cheeks wouldn't have gapped any barber's razor, but a young blood, right on the edge of being a man, gets a big lift out of sprawling back in a chair and getting his face soaped and scraped. Even if the hair lining his jawbone doesn't amount to much more than peach fuzz.

They crawled into the barbershop bathtubs to soak away the grime and sweat. They climbed into brand-new town-going garments that had set them back a couple of months' wages. Calfskin boots with toothpick toes and big butterflies ornamenting the high tops. Swank britches, creased to a razor edge. Big, wide, hand-tooled leather belts with silver buckles set with rubies and diamonds. The rubies and diamonds weren't real, but who could tell the difference? White boiled shirts and candy-striped neckties. Creamy white ten-gallon hats with bands of braided horsetail hairs. Mac wore a hatband made from the hide of a rattlesnake.

With those hats set on their heads at a go-to-hell slant, they crawled into the sky-blue roadster, gunned the motor, and quit that little old one-horse town of Alpine in a fog of dust.

Look out, Big City girls! Here come three bold, bad cowhands from off the range!

They put up in the biggest hotel in El Paso. They sent a bellboy after a bottle of bootleg whiskey. They drank it straight, using the gulp-and-shudder method, because no real he-cowhand will put up with having his whiskey watered down, for she-fashion drinking.

42

They went down to a swank dining room and ordered meals that cost them a day's wages. Then they went back up to drink some more, before Bunion demanded of Mac, "Where's all them girls you been bragging about having lined up?"

As it turned out, Mac didn't have any girls lined up. All he had was an old aunt living in town; she might know some girls.

Bunion was disgusted and scornful. "Well, get on the telephone," he ordered. "You promised us girls, and girls is what we're after."

That aunt of Mac's, for a woman of sixty, she was a surprise job. She told Mac to come right on over, that she'd have the girls there. And she did. Pretty girls. Pretty as a picture on one of them New Year calendars. Full of fun, too.

The only trouble was, they were *nice* girls. At least, that's the way the young cowhands figured them. They were girls just like their sisters; and any one of those boys knew damned well their sisters were *nice* girls. And nice girls were not what these three cowhands were looking for. You don't fool around with nice girls; you marry them. And right now, marrying wasn't what these three had on their minds.

"Well, confound it!" Bunion swore, after they'd enjoyed the company of the nice girls and finally taken them home. "I can beat that."

"Where?" Mac said.

"I'll show you," Bunion said.

And he did. He hunted around town for a while and finally dug up three girls as pretty as a man could ask for. Prettier, in a way, even than those *nice* girls. They

43

were quicker to like a man, too, seemed like. The only
trouble was, with a background and upbringing like
Fat's, the whole business made him feel sort of cheap
and low-down.

The next day, they got caught. Mac had parked out
under some cottonwoods alongside an irrigation ditch,
not far enough out of town or far enough off the road.
He could have driven twenty feet further around some
salt cedar bushes and been out of sight. But no, he had
to have that flashy roadster parked right out in the
broad open, where a nearsighted duck could have recognized them a mile off.

Mac and Bunion were up in the front seat with their
girls. They were explaining that there very likely wasn't
another set of cowhands in the whole West as big and
strong and handsome and wild-riding as the three in
the car. It happened to be Fat's turn in the back seat
right then, and he was busy telling his girl pretty much
the same story.

And that's when Mac's aunt drove up, to park right
beside them.

There's no way of describing how awful an old country boy can feel at a time like that. Fat wished he could
sink right through that grandma seat. He wished he
could crawl into a varmint hole and pull the hole in
after him. He wished he could just up and die, right
there, quick, before he had to suffer any more shame.
He wished he hadn't even been born.

He pushed the girl down out of sight and scrooged
down beside her till there was nothing left exposed but
the bridge of his humped nose. But he knew it was no

use. He knew he'd already been seen, and the shame of it weakened every bone in his body.

Mac's aunt was old, but she sure wasn't blind. She had to have seen those girls there in the car. She couldn't have helped it. But if she did, she didn't seem to take any notice. She just smiled and said, "Saw your car out here and stopped by to invite you all out to supper to-night. It'll be ready about seven." Then she drove away.

There was no more love-making after that. No more braggy whiskey talk or warm cuddling or girl-giggling. That was all done and over with.

A moment ago, the swank blue roadster had held three bold, proud cowhands, each one of them a proved woman-killer. Now, all it held was three ignorant guilt-sick country boys who could hardly wait to get back to town and dump their women.

The girls looked puzzled, disappointed, and a little hurt; but nobody bothered to explain anything to them.

Fat trailed Mac and Bunion up to the hotel room. All the strut and pride was out of their walk. Castrate a couple of stray dogs, and they wouldn't have looked any sorrier or sicker. Fat felt just like they looked.

Up in the room, Mac and Bunion started changing to clean clothes, getting ready to go eat supper with Mac's aunt. Fat squirmed at the prospect. Speaking mighty offhand and casual, he made a brave try for escape.

"Boys," he said, "I don't much believe I'll go with you tonight. My stomach ain't feeling just right. Must be that old whiskey we drunk."

Mac was bent over, digging some shorts out of his suitcase, his long bony frame as naked as a plucked jay-bird. Bunion had on his hat and a fresh shirt and was

45

sitting in a chair, pulling on his boots. Both stopped what they were doing to hand Fat the hardest, most accusing stares Fat ever tried to face down.

"Whiskey, my eye!" Mac flared. "The trouble with your stomach is the same thing that's troubling mine. And it sure ain't whiskey."

Then Bunion spoke up in a dead-level voice that was even more threatening. "Listen, Frog Legs," he said. "You're in this just as deep as we are. And when Mac's aunt gets up there in her house tonight and starts raking us over the coals, you're going to be standing right with us, hearing up your part of it!"

The supper Mac's aunt dished out that night was the kind to make a cowhand's mouth water. She served as pretty a table of fine fixings as Fat ever laid an eye on. And right there across the table sat those three nice girls again, just as pretty and fun-loving as ever.

Fat kept asking himself why the old lady had invited those girls over at a time like this. Did she aim to haul him and Mac and Bunion on the carpet right in front of them!

The prospect made Fat's senses reel. His face got hot. His collar choked off his wind. He had to pick up his grub and stuff a little down, for show. But for taste, he'd just as soon have been eating sawdust. He sneaked a glance at Mac and Bunion. They weren't saying anything. They weren't eating anything, either. Just picking at their grub, the same as Fat, and looking sick enough to've just swallowed a dose of salts.

Fat kept wondering why the old lady didn't go ahead and get it over with, and died a thousand deaths waiting for her to start.

46

And every death was wasted. Because the aunt never said a word about it all evening, and if she ever did afterward, the three bold, woman-killing cowhands from off the range never learned of it.

The day before they got caught, Fat had got to thinking some about nice girls and girls not so nice. And, there for a while, he'd got to wondering if there was any real difference, other than one was more willing than the other. And he'd sort of wondered if the nice girls might have been a little more willing, themselves, if anybody had given them a chance. And he'd thought maybe he might give them a chance the next time.

Only, of course, as low-down and cheap as he'd felt that last night, he wasn't in any mood to talk anybody out of anything. So he never did learn whether his theory was any good or not.

8

AS Seth Fry, the Elsinore rider, pointed out when Fat roped the muley cow, any cowboy worth his salt had a rope hand that itched clear up to his elbow. Seth claimed that the urge to rope something is as natural to a cowhand as crying is to a woman.

Seth held a reputation for stretching the blanket at times, but the fact remains that most cowhands are forever practicing the art of roping like they planned to win the world championship next week. Roping is an occupational disease with them, and one that cattle owners are forever and vainly trying to cure; chousing and roping and dragging down cattle is not a way to help them put on weight. But trying to cure a working cowhand of indiscriminate roping is like trying to break a boy of baseball fever. The patient isn't interested. The cowhand takes pride in making catches under difficult circumstances and likes to brag about having roped just about any and everything that ever jumped and ran from him.

Judged by this standard, Fat was a born cowhand. His roping fever had burned at a high temperature ever since he was a patch-seated kid. First he'd roped fence posts and stumps and chickens and pigs and milk calves. Then, after he'd got old enough to ride a horse, he'd teamed up with a boy named Jack Kidwell, near Valera, Texas, and really put his heart into practicing.

It was Jack Kidwell who first called him Fat, the name he was to wear for the rest of his life. That was after Fat had recovered from a long spell of sickness and his runty body had suddenly started filling out to man size.

Jack was the son of a preacher and, like many preachers' sons, felt that he had to be a little wilder than other boys to offset the piousness of his parent.

The boys did most of their roping on Sundays. Jack would wait till his father had gone off to preach, then he'd get on the telephone and call Fat. Fat would saddle a horse and tie on his catch-rope and meet Jack at a designated spot. From there, they'd ride around till they located the cattle of some churchgoing rancher. Then they'd take down their ropes and get at it.

They'd each spur his horse after a different animal, competing to see who could rope, throw, and tie down his catch in the shortest time. Each tied one end of his rope to his saddle horn, held the coil of slack rope in his left hand, and swung his loop with his right. He'd ride up on the left side of the running cow, toss his loop over her horns or neck, and jerk her down. And before she could get up, he'd be out of the saddle and on her, grabbing up a foreleg and hauling back on it so she couldn't get to her feet. Then, with his other hand and one foot to help, he'd cross the cow's other three feet and tie them together with the pigging string he held in his teeth.

Sometimes, if it was a big cow that he didn't figure his horse could hold, he'd rope her, then throw her by pitching the slack of his rope back of the animal's heels and running his horse against it. This would generally roll her. Then, if the roper was quick enough, he could be on her before she could get to her feet, and by pulling her tail up tight between her hind legs he could usually hold her down long enough to get her tied.

They practiced "heeling" and "forefooting," too, and after they got good at laying a loop out right to pick up a running steer's hind or forefeet, they got too lazy to want to bother with tying an animal, then having to turn it loose; so they practiced "tiptoeing." Each boy got so he could ride up beside the animal he wanted to catch, reach over her back, and pick up her forefeet from the off side, then wheel his horse away at such an angle that, when the cow went down, she also rolled clear over on her back. That way, while the cow was still rolling, the roper could give a little slack, and the cow would generally kick free of the loop, saving him the bother of having to dismount and turn her loose.

It was good practice for kids who were to become working cowhands, even if they didn't have that in mind at the time. It gave them a sure command of those essentials of roping: a sense of rhythm, a sense of timing, and the ability to gauge distances.

Some men claim that the ability to rope comes from practice only; but after years of experience, Fat doesn't hold with that theory. He can name you cowhands who spent a lifetime trying to learn the art and still can't get a rope on a horse standing still in a fence corner. Some of them, he says, can hardly pitch a loop out on the ground and run off and leave it there.

But Fat was lucky. He was born with what it takes to make a good rope hand. With that start, and with the practice he got with his friend Jack Kidwell, he made

50

himself into as good a roper as ever caught a cow out of the brush.

Working cowhands use all sorts of ropes, from the cable-hard one woven of sisal hemp to the eight-strand Mexican lariat of braided rawhide strips. Lengths of ropes vary from the short thirty-footer generally favored by the South Texas brush-popper to the extreme lengths of sixty and seventy feet that some of the old-time Great Plains riders used for dally work (meaning that they wrapped the ends of their ropes around the saddlehorn to hold a roped animal, in contrast to the "tie-hard" ropers, such as Fat, who preferred their ropes tied fast to their saddlehorns at all times).

Fat always looked upon these extra long ropes as "brag ropes." The only man he ever saw who could catch a cow at the end of a long rope was Roy Babb, who used to ride for the Block Y outfit, and Babb's rope was only a forty-five-footer.

Most ropers, including Fat, used a thirty-two- to thirty-five-foot rope, and swung a fairly good-sized loop. A few went to extremes in loop sizes, from the big, slow-traveling Community Loop that "tried to take in all of Creation," to the little Bird's Nest that whistled with speed but had better be thrown as straight as a bullet, since it was built to fit, with no room to spare.

Fat himself used what in West Texas was termed a Morning Glory Loop, one of fairly good size, and thrown in such a way that it opened just as it got there. And given his choice of ropes, he took the yellow, four-strand, silk manila rope, called a "whale line," that, before the last war, was manufactured by the Plymouth Cordage Company.

For Fat and for most American cowhands, this silk rope topped all others for strength, durability, and, most important of all, for "live touch," there being nothing a roper detests worse than a "dead" rope.

With a good horse between his legs and a "live whale line" in his hands, Fat figured himself equal to any roper on horseback. In fact, he considered himself so good that after he'd started working as a cowhand in the trans-Pecos country, he almost got his feelings hurt one day when a cowboy by the name of Howard Capps opened his eyes to what a man could do with a rope.

Fat and Howard were riding a pasture, hunting out and doctoring wormy sheep. Howard rode in the lead, following around the rim of a box canyon. This canyon was shaped like a horseshoe and had solid walls of rock dropping sheer away from the rim. It was maybe twenty feet to the bottom, and the walls were so smooth they looked like somebody had used a pick to cut them into shape. Little scrub-sized oak grew out of the rock-littered ground on top.

Up out of this brush came a ewe. In the top of her back was a bloody wormhole big enough for a man to shove his fist into; but she was still spry. There were goat and sheep trails leading in all directions, and she took to the one leading around the rim of this box canyon. She was running fast.

Howard hooked spurs to his horse and downed his rope. The sheep was running on his left, the wrong side for roping, but Howard couldn't move the horse over. The edge of that cliff was too close under him.

Howard was pulling up close; his horse's feet were knocking loose rocks off into the canyon, and the old ewe knew she was fixing to get caught. She whipped left and took a long leap out into thin air.

Well, that would have stopped most cowhands, but not Howard Capps. He just stood in his stirrups, leaned 'way over in his saddle, and let fly.

The sheep was about halfway to the bottom and falling fast when Howard's loop snaked out and stood wide open under her. She fell into it. Howard jerked up his slack—and had him a sheep caught.

She was still hanging against the wall and blatting when Fat rode up. Howard started pulling her to the top, hand over hand.

"Come out of there, sheep," Howard was saying. "You can't get away from me. I'll just draw you up like you was a bucket of water out of a well."

That's when Fat came to the reluctant conclusion that there were some other mighty good ropers besides himself. He might argue that Howard's roping the sheep had been a plain accident, but the fact remained that Howard had roped it.

A thing like that is hard on a man who takes pride in his own ability as a roper, and it was some time before Fat managed to pull off a couple of roping feats to measure up to that one of Howard's.

The first happened on a cow hunt in Johnson Draw, down near Juno. This was rough country, with cedars standing tall as a man on a horse and so thick they whipped a rider blind when he got in a hurry. There

53

were eight or ten riders in all, working for Wayne West under Mark Rogers. Nobody had located a cow yet; if cattle were in the cedars, they were drifting out ahead of the riders.

Suddenly Fat heard a yell and a clatter of hoofs. He looked up a steep slant. Here came Mark Rogers and a rider named Carson, right off the hill onto him. They came busting through the cedars, hollering like their shirttails were afire, hard after a big coyote.

The wolf was ducking and dodging through the brush, and Rogers and Carson were wasting one loop after another, trying to catch him. But the brush was too thick.

Fat was mounted on an old broomstick of a horse with a lot of mane and tail and not much in between. The only thing about this horse that Fat could depend on was that he would run away. But, horse or no horse, when Fat got a glimpse of that big coyote loping down through the cedars, he had to get in on the chase. A wolf was one thing he'd never yet roped.

He roweled the cold steel to his broomstick pony and all but lifted him to the top of a caving caliche bank, where he figured to cut the wolf off.

But the wolf saw him in time and turned down a deep wash, closer to Rogers and Carson. They spurred in after him, ahead of Fat now, and it looked like Fat was going to lose out.

That draw was a long one and dipped mighty fast. Going down it, the fast-running horses picked up a lot more speed than they could well handle on such rough ground. Mark and Carson saw the wolf come to the end of the draw and leap over the edge of a cut bank that dropped straight down some ten or twelve feet. Carson hauled back on his reins, rump-sliding his horse to a halt at the brink. Rogers, a more reckless rider, tried to force his mount to take the leap, but the horse wouldn't.

Carson hollered, "We can't git off here!"

But Fat was just behind, riding hell for leather on his old broomstick that was so hot and mad by now that he was running wild and blind. "The devil you can't," he shouted. "I'll fix that!" The next instant, his runaway horse slammed into Carson's, knocking him clean off the bluff and leaping over him as he fell.

The yelling Carson and his horse piled up in the bed of the cut, but Fat's broomstick landed right side up, and still running. Right ahead of Fat, within roping distance now, went the wolf, bound for the tall cedars again. Fat reached out with a loop built to fit and laid it on him.

The broomstick, still running blind, dragged the wolf a good long piece before he ran head on into a cedar and stopped.

Fat rode back to the cut, with Broomstick wringing his tail and fighting the bits till the blood dripped off his chin. Circling them was the big wolf, snarling and snapping and making high jumps into the air to get free of the rope.

Carson and his horse had got to their feet by this time. Carson didn't much appreciate the way Fat had run over him and knocked him off the bluff; so when he saw that Fat had roped the wolf he'd aimed to catch, he spoke up, claiming it had been a pure accident, that Fat couldn't rope that wolf again in a dozen throws.

Fat was indignant. "Carson," he said firmly, "if you got the least little doubt in your mind that this wolf roping was an accident, we'll just turn him loose right now and start all over again."

But just then Mark Rogers ran up beside the wolf with a club and knocked him in the head, ruining Fat's chance to prove that the roping had been no accident.

The second roping feat that Fat gets a lot of fun out of bragging about happened the time he and Dave Poole were camped out at a windmill on the Neville ranch.

Fat and Dave had turned a couple of mounts out to graze, and these horses had drifted off and joined a bunch of half-wild stuff running loose in country so rough that a man could hardly get them out. Off and on for weeks, they'd been trying to pen these horses and catch up their mounts; but all they'd managed to do so far was chouse the bunch around and make them wilder than ever.

Then, one evening just at sundown, they happened onto the whole band, out in the open where they could ride around and cut them off from the roughs.

Dave said, "Now, where can we pen 'em?"

"Well, the only place I know," Fat said, "is that old wire pen across yonder at the windmill."

"Why, Fat," Dave said. "That little old pen's just hanging to the stars; it wouldn't hold me if I was to run agin it, real scared."

"I know, but maybe if we'll just drift 'em in real easy, they won't break out before we can get ropes on them two we want."

56

So they started working the wild ones toward the wire pen, keeping a long way behind, taking their time, hiding behind bushes and rocks, doing everything they knew how to keep the horses moving in the right direction without scaring them into a run.

They finally made it, just about nightfall. The horses went into the pen. Fat got off his horse and sneaked up and shut the gate.

"Now," Fat told Dave, "we ain't going to get but one throw apiece before them crazy ones bust out of here; so you ease up and lay your best loop on one of them we want. I'll be on the far side, all cocked and primed to catch the other'n as they come through."

It was getting so dark by this time that about the only way a man could recognize one horse from the other was to squat down low and skylight him. So Dave got down and crawled through the wires into the pen and searched the bunch till he'd located one of the horses they wanted and let fly with his rope.

The sound of Dave's rope whipping through the air kicked the lid off. There was wild snorting and a clatter of hoofs, and here they went, some through the fence and some over it, with rotten fence posts cracking and popping and wires screeching through the staples, and the thick dust fogging high in the last pale light of the evening.

Fat, on the other side of the pen, was all set for them. He stood with his loop ready, while the horses came crashing through. He caught sight of the nose of one high-lunging horse and that nose looked familiar. So he reached out and laid on with his rope, then fell back against it, digging his boot heels into the hard ground.

It didn't do much good. He'd stood on the ground and roped and held many a horse, but it seemed like this one was more than a match for him. It dragged him off through the darkness, with his boot heels plowing up furrows in the dirt as if his weight amounted to nothing.

He yelled at Dave, "You get your'n?" and Dave said, "Hell, no. I missed!"

"Well, come get on this rope with me. I got one, but he's fixing to drag me plumb out of the country."

Dave came running through the hole the horses had knocked in the pen. "No wonder you can't hold him," he shouted, as he added his weight to Fat's rope. "You got two horses!"

"Well, the way they're pulling," Fat said, "I figured I'd caught a dozen."

When they finally brought the lunging horses to a halt, Dave was the first one to go up the rope. He got his hands on the horses, then stood silent a moment before breaking into soft and profane utterances.

"What's the matter?" Fat wanted to know.

"You," he said wonderingly, "have caught both them horses we wanted."

Fat recovered from his surprise and demanded, "And what's wrong with that?"

"There ain't nothing wrong with it," Dave said. "I was just thinking what a big accident it was that you roped the two we wanted in the same loop."

Fat's voice took on an injured tone. "What do you mean, accident? You missed your'n. That left me with two horses to catch with one loop. Ain't no accident to that kind of roping."

58

"You're a liar!" Dave flared. "Ain't nobody can stand in the dark and reach into a bunch of fifteen running horses and rope out the two he wants!"

Fat pointed at the horses. "I done it," he said. "And there's the proof."

But Dave wouldn't budge from his stand, and Fat would never admit that it had been an accident, and the two of them kept the argument going for days. Cowhands, out on the range that way, sometimes get pretty starved out for something to talk about.

Anyhow, Fat didn't figure catching the two horses they wanted in one loop was any more of an accident than Howard Capps's roping a sheep in mid-air!

9

EVERY five or six months, Fat would drift back home to pay his folks a visit. He always tried to be there for Christmas holidays. Seemed like Christmases were better, now that he was gone from home all the time; like maybe his family appreciated him more when he wasn't around so much.

The visit home during the third Christmas after he'd started working cattle didn't turn out so well, though. That was on account of his arrival's having been delayed by a Christmas Eve dance on the Colorado River.

He hadn't meant to stay at the dance any time. It was already dark when he'd run into it, and he was still four or five miles from home. But it was a cold ride he was making, and off the road there a piece was all this warm yellow lamplight shining through the windows and the sweet singing and crying of the fiddles and the thumping beat of the guitars and the measured stamp of dancers and the occasional whoop and holler of some young blood letting off steam. So he'd pulled off the road and ridden toward the house, aiming just to warm up and look on for a little while before making the last lap home.

But as it turned out, the celebrants took him in like he was a long-lost brother. They wined him and dined him. They introduced him to more pretty girls than he'd ever encountered before, all in a bunch. It wasn't

60

long till he was right out in the big middle of the celebration, having more fun than anybody.

Before it was over, he'd made a night of it, having won two fist-fights and the favor of a girl whose bold eyes had centered on him the moment he'd stepped into the house.

He arrived home shortly after daylight, his clothes rank with country-girl perfume and his eyes resembling a couple of fried eggs left too long after cooking.

His father had been young once and probably recognized the signs. Or it could have been that the grapevine was working good, as it generally is in country places. Anyhow, Julius Alford seemed to know exactly what had taken place the night before and felt dutybound to give his chunky son a sober lecture on the evils of strong drink and bad women.

He waited about delivering it, however, till the holidays were over and Fat was fixing to go back to work. Then he followed Fat down to the lot. There, while Fat was saddling his horse, the old man chewed on his Star Navy tobacco and gave it to Fat, hot and heavy.

Larence, Fat's older half-brother, was out there in the lot, pumping water into a trough, and it didn't help Fat's feelings any to have him standing there grinning and getting such a kick out of the way the old man was raking Fat up one side and down the other.

But Fat didn't say anything. He didn't figure it smart to pop off till he had his horse saddled. He just kept nodding and saying, "Yes, sir," and "No, sir," to the old man, as polite and respectful as he knew how, till he'd set his rig. He mounted and circled the pen a time or

61

two to walk the kinks out of the back of the gray horse he rode.

When he thought the gray was ready to travel without throwing a fit, he called on Larence to open the gate. He got set to ride, then twisted in his saddle to grin back at his father. "Dad," he asked, "man to man, now, didn't you ever get no fun out of messing around with the women?"

At the look on his dad's face, Fat hooked spurs to the big gray. They left out like they'd been shot at. But they weren't fast enough.

Julius Alford sent the first rock whizzing past his smart-alecky son Fat and grabbed up a fistful more. And the old man could throw a rock better than a lot of men can shoot a rifle.

Fat was spurring all the speed out of that gray horse that he could possibly get, but it still wasn't enough. One of the flying rocks struck the gray in the rump, and that was all the excuse the horse wanted. Right there he uncoupled himself and went off down the slant of the hill, pitching and weaving and grunting and bawling, doing everything but turning somersaults.

Fat never did lay claim to being a bronc-buster, but he's bragged more than one time about the ride he made that morning. But, as he always explains, his was a ground-hog case: it was climb a tree or the dog'll get you. For him, it was ride that horse or get piled up where the old man could reach him with those humming rocks.

Fat got himself a choke-hold on the saddle horn with one hand and grabbed a fistful of mane in the other and managed to stay with what he had till the gray finally threw up his tail and quit the country.

Larence told Fat later that the old man had stared for a long while at the trail dust Fat's horse left suspended in the air, then stalked back to the house and exploded to his wife. "That confounded son of yours, Alice, can make me the maddest of anybody I ever seen!"

Alice Alford didn't ask what it was all about. She just laughed, knowing that it wouldn't be but a few days till her husband would be bragging about something *his* boy Fat had done.

10

RETURNING to West Texas, Fat took up horse-breaking for a while. Not especially because he wanted to; for, as he explained to Mark Wilson, who hit him up in Ozona to take on a horsebreaking job, he'd been born shorthanded for bronc riding. A lot of riders made out fine with only two hands for pulling leather, but he wasn't one of them. He said he was generally in need of three or four extras when some high-rolling bronc set out to unload him.

But Wilson, who was boss for the Joe Blakeny outfit on Johnson Draw, claimed these horses weren't bad, just young stuff that had never been under a saddle. A man wouldn't have any real trouble with them, he said. So Fat took the job and learned that Wilson hadn't lied to him—much. Out of the ten head of broncs that Wilson turned over to him, Fat found only one that had any real craving to eat him alive.

This was a black horse. He wasn't big for size, but he had big ways. The first time Fat went into the pen, the black came running to welcome him; and before the reception was over, Fat was perched on the highest rail of the cedar-pole corral while down under him the black paced back and forth, with his ears laid back and his teeth bared, eying Fat like a hound dog watches a coon he's just treed.

Wilson came down to the corral about this time and

tried to tell Fat there wasn't any reason to fear the black. He said the short-coupled little devil was just bluffing, and he walked into the pen to prove it. But when the black wheeled and made a pantherlike lunge for him, Wilson squirreled up the side of the pole pen, just barely ahead of the black's chopping forefeet.

There the two of them sat, considering, while the black continued to pace below, snorting a little and keeping his war flag high, daring them to come down within reach.

A Mexican rider had been standing just outside the pen, watching the show from between the poles. Presently, he picked up a short length of cedar and pitched it out on the ground in front of the black. Fat and Wilson saw the horse whirl on that piece of wood and crunch it between his teeth like an angry bear. So the two of them sat right where they were and considered awhile longer.

Finally Fat decided that there wasn't much chance of breaking a horse to ride if they just kept sitting on the fence, watching him bite wood; so he climbed down on the outside of the corral and saddled another horse and rode him inside. When the black made a bare-toothed run at them, Fat swung his mount aside and picked up the black's forefeet in his loop.

He wasn't too gentle about letting the black to the ground, and he made sure the animal stayed there by backing his horse off and keeping the rope tight, so the black couldn't get his feet to the ground.

He held him on his side till the Mexican brought a saddle and cinched it up tight on the black. Then he climbed down off his horse and stepped across, as the Mexican let the black to his feet.

The black tried hard. He came up, bawling his rage, pitching hard and high. But this was his first experience with bucking, and he couldn't seem to get the right sort of warp in his backbone to give a rider the head-popping jolters a lot of horses do. At that, Fat was beginning to wish for at least one extra hand before the black finally gave up and stood stock-still, with his barrel heaving and his leg muscles quivering.

Fat stepped off then. But if he hadn't been the fastest short-legged cowhand afoot, he'd never have made it to the fence in time.

Fat rode the black three or four saddles there in the pen with the Mexican helping him. Then, one day as he mounted, he called for the gate to be thrown open.

The black didn't have to be told about it. This was what he'd been waiting for. Maybe he couldn't unload his rider by pitching, but he had some other tricks in mind. He shot through the gate like he couldn't wait, and went yonder.

There was a four-wire fence between him and the wide-open spaces, and he headed straight for it like it wasn't there. Fat hauled back so hard on the hackamore, trying to turn him, that he had the black's nose pulled around beside his left leg. So the black opened his mouth and seized Fat's leg and was busy trying to bite it in two when he hit the fence.

The wires squawled and some posts snapped off, but, at the pace they were traveling, no four-wire fence could stop them. They went through, or over, Fat wasn't sure which; but the fence broke the black's

66

tooth-grip on Fat's leg. So Fat gave the black his head, thinking to let him run himself down.

By all rights, the black should have—or killed his fool self. They were out in some hills that were high and rocky and rough, and it didn't stand to reason that a horse running as fast and wild as this one could last long, or even keep his feet under him. But the black did. He kept right on, up the side of one hill and down the other, jumping boulders and running into scrub trees and slipping and half falling on slick flat rocks, but always coming up to run some more.

Finally, out there ahead of them was the rimrock of a bluff some fifteen feet high. The black could see just as plain as Fat could that there was a drop-off there, but he headed right for it and Fat couldn't turn him.

Right then, if Fat had been using his head, he'd have stepped off and let the black take the jump alone. But by this time he was so hot and mad, and his chewed leg was paining him so, that his temper was up. He swore at the black, telling him that if he didn't have no more sense than to jump off that bluff, that he didn't have no more sense than to go off with him.

So off they went.

Fat doesn't know of another thing that'll raise the hair on a man's head like riding a wild-running horse off a fifteen-foot bluff. It seemed to him like they dropped through the air for five minutes before they landed. But they hit straight up and still running, so it was all right.

Well, this was just the beginning of the fight between Fat and the black, and that fight went on day after day. The black had himself a whole bag of such tricks, and he tried them all, but finally settled down mainly to one he'd used on that first wild run—leg biting.

His neck was short and thick, but it was sure surprising how quick he could whip his head around for a grab at Fat's leg. Fat was watching him all the time and still couldn't always escape.

Finally, Fat got right down on the same level with the black and gave him back some of his own medicine. Every time the black bit his leg, Fat would reach up and grab one of the black's ears and bite him back.

But it didn't do a lot of good. The fight between the two continued, clear up to the time Fat finished with the rest of the horses and turned them back to Wilson.

By then, Fat and the black had come to more or less of an understanding. Fat could saddle and mount him, and the black wasn't running and pitching and jumping off as many high places as he had at first. But Fat's leg was still sore and the black's ears had been bitten till the tips of them were permanently bent. And Fat still couldn't do any cow work on him, to speak of.

Best Fat could judge, the fight wound up as just a fair draw. He sure wouldn't want to say that the black was a well-broken cow horse when he turned him back to Wilson.

Not all horses are as stubborn and hard to manage as that leg-biting black, but saddle breaking even the meekest of the young ones isn't a job to be left to the womenfolks and children.

Any horse that has been left to run wild and free is terrified by men, ropes, and saddles, and the animal's first acquaintance with such is going to bring out all the fight that's in him.

The breaking usually starts when a pony is a three-year-old. As Fat points out, a horse younger than that generally isn't tough enough to take the harsh treatment the peeler will give him; while if he's left till he's four or better, the chances are he'll be tough enough to give the peeler more harsh treatment than he can stand.

Theories on horsebreaking are as numerous and varied as the men who do it, but once the fancy extras are skimmed off, the procedure boils down to about the method that Fat used.

When Fat took on a bunch of young ones to break, generally ten or twelve head at a time, he'd first run them into a corral where he could rope and put hackamores on them and start getting them used to the rope. The hackamore is made of soft rope and amounts to about the same thing as a bridle, with one exception—it has no steel bits. The bits would tear up a young bronc's mouth before he could learn not to fight them.

Getting that hackamore over the bronc's head sometimes calls for some doing, what with the frightened horse rearing and snorting and chopping at a man with his front feet, hoping to cave in his skull.

But where the big fight usually takes place is with the first saddling. An experienced bronc-peeler can generally get a good grip on a fighting bronc's ear, hold him with that hand, keep out of the way of his flailing front hoofs, and still saddle him with the other hand. But if the horse gets too rambunctious, the peeler may have to rope his forefeet, throw him, then saddle him while he's on the ground.

This procedure calls for tying the bronc's feet together so he can't get up, laying the saddle upside down on the ground behind him, rolling the bronc over till his back's in the saddle, then holding him there till the girth can be pushed around and cinched tight.

Once that's done, the rest is real simple. All the peeler has to do is stand astraddle of the bronc, while he releases the animal's feet. The bronc rolls up, lifting the man with him. If the man's quick enough, he can get his seat in the saddle and both feet in the stirrups. And then, if he's the kind who can keep his balance astride a prairie cyclone, he can give this bronc a first taste of what it's like to pack a man on his back.

Some riders prefer to tie up one hind leg of the bronc. With only three feet on the ground, the bronc can't put up much of a fight while the saddle's being cinched to his back. But Fat never did think much of this method. He said it was his experience that the bronc with a tied-up foot generally took the wall-eyed fits and threw himself to the ground anyhow; and, on top of that, often wound up with a rope burn back of his hind foot bad enough to cripple him. And once a bronc that's been messed with gets crippled till he has to be turned out for a while, he's nine times harder to break on the second go-around.

Fat liked to keep his "rough string," as horses being broken are usually called, staked out on a long rope tied to a drag. This drag might be a log or a rock or almost anything not tied down but still heavy enough that a young bronc couldn't get far with it. This gave the raw

one a chance to work off a lot of steam, fighting and running against the rope, without doing himself any real
injury, till he finally caught onto the fact that the rope
had him whipped. Once the bronc learned this hard
truth, Fat could usually untie the drag and lead the
animal wherever he pleased.

Fat's special trick for getting a bronc used to the
bridle bits was to bridle him right at the start, remove
the reins, and let the horse wear the bridle continuously
for maybe a couple of weeks. Fat still used a hackamore
for handling the bronc; all the bridle was for was to give
the bronc a chance to get used to the bits in his mouth
before the time came for them to be used.

After about thirty days of being saddled and ridden
once a day, a bronc generally has enough of the rough
edges knocked off him to be ready for cow work. That
is, if he's put to work right away. If not, a longer breaking period is necessary.

Also, after about thirty days of wrestling with a raw
string of ten or twelve horses, the peeler's minus a good
lot of hide, and stove up enough to feel like he's earned
at least a good part of the pay he draws.

Fat broke one bunch of horses belonging to Will Baggett, who ranched for years in the Ozona country.
Among West Texas cowhands, it was pretty well agreed
that you couldn't work for a better man than Will Baggett. He paid wages to equal anybody's, and, on top of
that, treated a cowhand like he was a human being. He
wasn't always asking for the impossible, like some.

He treated his foreman Theodore Short the same

71

way; but Short was the worrying kind, always afraid he wouldn't quite get things done to suit his boss.

Baggett drove Fat out to the ranch and told him, "Now, Mr. Short's foreman here, so you take orders from him."

That was all right with Fat. He didn't figure he'd need a lot of orders to get a bunch of horses broken.

And Short didn't give him many. About all he did was hang to Fat's shirttail, watching every move he made with those horses, rubbing his hands together, frowning and muttering, worrying about whether or not Fat was doing the job right.

Short was a fine old man, and Fat liked him a lot; but the way Short kept worrying got on Fat's nerves. He knew Baggett, and knew that if he did a halfway decent job of horsebreaking, Baggett wasn't going to raise a fuss about it.

Some of these horses had been pretty badly bent, but they sure hadn't been broken. One was a sorrel that looked to Fat like he might set a man off to picking flowers if he wasn't handled easy and watched close. When the day came for him to saddle this sorrel, Fat led him out of the main pen. Baggett had blasted that pen out of solid rock, and it didn't provide the most comfortable landing ground. Fat took the sorrel into an adjoining pen that had a few rock ribs sticking up, all right; but at least there was some dirt between them that a man might be lucky enough to fall on.

Short was hovering around, worrying, as usual. He trailed in behind Fat and the sorrel, not right sure but what Fat might be doing the wrong thing to swap pens this way.

72

Fat paid him no mind. He had this sorrel figured for a bad one and was watching the horse's every move. He climbed aboard, all set for some high riding—and the sorrel just stood there, apparently not even resenting him.

Fat touched the sorrel with a spur, still not quite convinced. The sorrel stepped right out, following behind Short, who was now headed for the gate. Short was still rubbing his hands together and shaking his head about Fat's swapping pens. And that's when Fat decided that if the old man enjoyed worrying so much, he'd try to give him something to worry about. He slammed the Kelly Rogers to the sorrel, and this surprise move exploded the horse into action. He headed straight for Short, bawling and pitching.

Short broke into a run. The walls of the pen were high and built of bull wire, and the gates were low to the ground, so that there wasn't any place for him to go except around the pen. Which he did, at a pretty spry pace for a man his age. The sorrel went right in after him, following him like a dog would a cat, as if maybe Short was the one who'd roweled him with those spurs.

As it turned out, the sorrel could pitch about like Fat had him figured to; so, what with being so tickled at how fast the old man was scampering about, Fat blew a stirrup and was grabbing for the horn when Short suddenly dived under a gate so low to the ground that Fat wouldn't have thought a scared rabbit could have made it.

But Short did, and came up on the other side with alarm widening his eyes.

"Goshamighty!" he gasped. "He like to've got me!"

73

Fat had already picked himself out a place between some rocks to fall, but the sorrel stopped there at the gate. So Fat pulled himself back up in the saddle and was just as concerned as he could be by the old man's narrow escape.

"Well, now, he sure did, Mr. Short," he said innocently.

In that same bunch of horses was a bronc that Fat kept putting off to ride, knowing that the animal was too big and clumsy to be worth anything as a cow horse.

To Fat's way of thinking, a good cow horse didn't need to weigh more than a thousand to eleven hundred pounds, and those pounds needed to be in the right places. What Fat and most cowhands wanted in a horse was one that was trim, leggy, well set up, with a strong back, a big lung capacity, and heavy rump muscles to give him speed and driving power. He needed a clear-footed gait and the ability to keep his balance, whether on three feet or one. On top of that, he needed a fighting spirit that would keep him pushing beyond his strength, and a toughness of body that would allow him to take a spill and come back on his feet, still all in one piece.

Best Fat could tell, this big horse Short wanted him to ride had these last two important qualities, but mighty few of the others. Fat would have turned him out and sold him for a plow horse. But Short wouldn't have it. Baggett had said he wanted all these young horses broken to ride, and that big horse had been in the bunch when he'd said it; Fat would just have to break him, too.

Finally, Fat gave up arguing and saddled the big

74

horse. The animal didn't offer to pitch; all he wanted to do was run. Fat tried him with a hackamore and couldn't hold him; then he tried a bridle. Finally, he rode him with both; but still, any time the horse made up his mind to run, he ran.

There was lots of work to be done on the ranch, and Fat helped with it as much as he could on those scary broncs. One day, mounted on this big runaway, he rode with Short to a windmill where they found a wormy ewe with a lamb, hanging around the watering trough. Short told Fat to rope the ewe and he'd catch the lamb; so Fat made a run at the sheep and picked her up in his loop. But after he'd done it, he couldn't get the big horse to stop running till after he'd dragged the ewe to death against the rocks and brush.

This made Fat mad and proved his point that the horse wouldn't be any good for stock work; but it nearly worried old man Short to death. Here they'd lost a good ewe and were left with a dogie lamb that might die, too, if they couldn't get another ewe to mother it. What on earth could he tell Mr. Baggett?

Fat made the suggestion that Short tell Baggett the truth and let it go at that. He pointed out that, as long as Baggett had been ranching, he'd more than likely happened to an accident or two himself. But passing the accident off that way would have left Short with nothing to worry about; so he kept shaking his head and wondering if he should try to explain it this way to Mr. Baggett or some other, and what did Fat think? He kept this up till they'd ridden to another watering place, where they found a wormy cow that needed doctoring. She was a big cow, and Fat hated to see an old man tie

75

onto something heavy; so he told Short to let him do the roping.

"But that horse might drag her to death, too," the old man protested. "Then what could we tell Mr. Baggett?"

"Well, I aim to fix it so that won't happen," Fat said.

He got down and tied his rope around the runaway's neck and took a half hitch around the horse's head above the bits. Then he got back on and spurred after the cow.

For a big horse, this one could cover ground pretty fast. Wasn't but a little bit till he had Fat up in reach of the cow. Fat tied on.

Then he stepped to the ground, leaving the big horse to the mercy of the cow.

The runaway horse passed up that cow like a freight train passing a tramp. This turned the cow so that she was running in almost the opposite direction when the slack went out of the rope between them. And, with the horse tied up like he was, the cow had all the advantage. She stood the runaway on his head, flattened him to the ground, and dragged him a little piece before his weight stopped her. Then she came back and ran on the rope in another direction and dragged him some more.

By the time Fat and old man Short got to them, the cow had that half hitch pulled up so tight around the runaway's head that he couldn't get up and could just barely draw in a breath.

Mr. Short was terribly alarmed. "Why, he's smothering to death, Fat! What'll we do?"

"Why, I think I can bring him to, all right, Mr. Short," Fat said.

"Well, hurry, then," the old man ordered. "I just wouldn't know what to tell Mr. Baggett if we killed one of his horses."

So Fat hurried, like Mr. Short said, and broke off a dead but solid mesquite club and went to work on the big iron-jawed runaway. He whammed him across the rump several heavy licks, then went up and applied the club to the horse's jaw for a while. After that, he got slack in the rope and let the horse to his feet.

All this was so startling and unexpected to old man Short that he just sat there in his saddle and didn't open his worried head one time.

How Short ever got it all explained to Mr. Baggett, Fat never did learn; but he didn't see how Baggett could complain. After that round, anybody who aimed to rope anything off that bronc had sure better be screwed down tight in his saddle when he made his throw. Because that big runaway could stop, squat, and brace himself against the roped animal so fast that a man could hardly stay in the saddle.

After that, pitching a loop past his head was just like running him head on against a solid rock wall.

11

LIKE most working cowhands, Fat broke a lot of horses here and yonder, and did a fair job of it. He could ride the pitch out of most of them, train them to rein, teach them how to stop and throw a roped cow, and how to help a rider hold that cow down by backing off and keeping a tight rope on her. But he never acquired the knack of breaking and gentling them, like some. Not, for instance, like a rider who went by the name of Tiger.

There was a bronc-rider for you—that Tiger. An all-round cowhand, for that matter. But mostly he broke horses because he was such an artist at it that he never got time to do much else.

Tiger was a character. Long, tall rider, thin as a split rail. Fill him full of whiskey, and he still wouldn't weigh more than a hundred and a half. He was a confirmed bachelor, and proud of the fact. He claimed to have pure English blood in his veins, and did some bragging about that. Tiger would make friends with you or fight you like a javelina hog, just however you wanted it. He was the wildest rider in West Texas, but could do a better job of breaking a horse gentle than any man Fat ever knew.

Fat rode with Tiger a while out on the 7N. The 7N was owned by the Hendersons, who hired a lot of Mexican help. These Mexicans were good riders, but they sometimes weren't as good as they needed to be to ride the sort of mounts the Hendersons furnished. Old outlaw horses that had been "rode at" just enough to be spoiled. Always hunting an excuse to shy at something and throw a rider clear into the Misty Beyond. And Tiger, having a wry, off-center brand of humor that might or might not have come with his English blood, could generally think of some innocent-looking way to throw those old Henderson horses into cloud-climbing spasms.

The 7N riders generally saddled and mounted in the pens; without hemming up those man-killing horses, they'd never have gotten saddles on them. And Tiger, he'd make it a habit to be on hand every morning at saddling time. He'd be inside the pen, messing around with his gear, stalling till the crew had fought their biting, kicking, snorting mounts to a standstill and got their saddles cinched on. Then, when everybody had finally climbed aboard and the corral gate was thrown open, here would come Tiger, headed for the horse he aimed to ride. He'd walk through that bunch of snorty horses, dragging his old hull of a saddle along the ground, right under their noses, and generally stumbling and falling over it about the time he got good in the middle of them.

That was always enough. That was exactly the sort of booger-move the horses were looking for. One would snort and bog his head, and that was a signal that the show was wide open to anybody who wanted to join, and they all did.

Out of the pen they'd come, in the wildest stampede of bawling and squealing and grunting and pitching that Fat ever laid eye to. Some would rear up and fall backwards, and some would run over others and knock them down, and some would quit the ground in high-rolling leaps that turned their bellies to the sun. Sometimes these sunfishers could warp their bodies around to land on their feet, and sometimes they couldn't. And roweling spurs would be clanking and the saddle leather popping, and men would be yelling and swearing in both English and Spanish.

And out in the big shouting, dust-fogged middle of it would stand Tiger, looking as startled and amazed as if he didn't have no idea of what it was all about or how it ever got started, but keeping an accurate count of unloaded riders by folding back a finger for each one as he hit the ground.

Tiger claimed the best count he ever got was eleven riders on the ground at one time, which happened to be every man mounted that morning. But later there was some argument about this, as one rider claimed that he hadn't been thrown at all, that he was still sitting tight in the saddle when his mount hit the ground; and he didn't figure it was any fault of his that the fool horse had all four feet sticking up in the air when he landed.

A lot of ranchers hearing about such tricks might think Tiger wasn't a very dependable cowhand; but when they hired him, they learned better. Tiger would go out on a job and do it right and stay longer than any man they could hire. It'd be months, sometimes a year—if the horsebreaking lasted that long—before Tiger would lay off from work and come to town.

But when he did, he went at his town-going in a way to make it count. He liked good whiskey, but that kind

80

was hard to get in Prohibition days; so he made out the best he could on the rotgut the bootleggers peddled. And around Ozona, where he usually came to town, it's generally conceded that he made out all right.

Like most cowhands, the first place he'd show up in town would be the barbershop, where he'd get the works. Bath, shampoo, haircut, shave, and any sweet-smelling tonic the barber might have on hand. But even by that time, he'd usually be several drinks along and with a bottle in his hip pocket to keep the cat from dying. And maybe he'd come in wagging a whole suitcase of dirty clothes he aimed to take to the laundry; but every now and then he'd be so far along by the time he got out of the barber chair that he'd forget what he meant to do with those dirty clothes. So he'd empty them out of the suitcase and stack them up on the sidewalk in front of the shop and go off and leave them there for a week or better. Unless somebody who knew him happened to gather them up and send them off to the laundry for him.

Whether he hit town with twenty dollars or two thousand—and sometimes he'd be packing that much wages in his pocket at one time—Tiger would stay till it was all gone. Seemed like he looked on having money in his pockets like some men do on having a disease: he couldn't rest till he'd gotten rid of it. And, of course, there were always plenty of women and bootleggers ready to go a long way out of their way to keep him happy.

But that was all right with Tiger. If they wanted it, they could have it, and so could any of the little old ragged kids running around town.

Sometimes he'd leave his hotel room, or wherever he happened to be staying, packing such a load that it took half the street for him to walk in. He'd maybe come across some little old patch-seated kid who hadn't seen a dime in six months. He'd holler at the kid and say, "Come on, kid. Let's go up here to the drugstore."

And he'd take that kid along and maybe pick up three or four more on the way and line them all up on the stools in front of the cold-drink fountain and not let a one leave till all were so stuffed with ice cream and sodas and candy that their eyeballs threatened to pop out of their heads. When the kids couldn't hold another bite, Tiger would grin and slap them all on the back and go weaving off in search of another drink.

He'd keep this sort of thing up, spending his money like it came pouring out of a pipe somewhere, till finally he'd wake up some morning without a penny left. Then he'd go look for whoever it was that'd been waiting for him to sober up and come break some horses, and that'd be the last anybody would see of him for six months or longer—and the last drink he'd take till he hit town again.

Nearly all cowhands hate the very idea of walking anywhere; but, according to Frank Polk, Tiger considered the act positively indecent. Frank used to turn out bench-made boots for Tiger and Fat and a lot of other West Texas cowhands, and he likes to tell about the time Tiger rode off from the 7N headquarters on a bronc pony that had never been under the saddle before. Tiger rode this pony into a deep, brush-clogged canyon late in the afternoon and got along fine till he happened to ride up too close on a deer lying in a thicket.

The frightened deer jumped to his feet and went bounding through the brush. This scared Tiger's mount. He went to pitching and running and running and pitching, and it seemed like he couldn't stop. Tiger could get him pulled up every now and then for a breather, but, quick as he'd rested a little, here the pony would go again.

Sundown came, and Tiger tried to get his mount headed back for the ranch, but the bronc wasn't interested. All he had in mind was to shed Tiger, and he went about it real serious. But Tiger didn't have the least notion of being set afoot by an old scrub pony that anybody could ride. So the contest went on and on.

Night came on, with the two of them still fighting through the live-oak brush in one canyon and then, to vary the thing a little, heading into a second canyon where the wild walnuts grew.

Now and then, Tiger would get the old pony pulled up and think maybe he could step down for a little rest; but every time he tried it, the bronc would take a scare and tear out for whichever dark canyon he wasn't in at the time.

When Tiger didn't show up back at headquarters that night, some of the riders got concerned, and, early the next morning, they went out to look for him. But they didn't get far up the canyon before they saw Tiger coming down it, his long, gangling figure as sloppy-looking in the saddle as ever.

When he got closer, though, they could see some difference in his looks, as well as the looks of his mount.

Both were skinned from head to foot and spattered with dried blood and had knots swelled up all over them from the beating they'd taken in the brush.

Of course, the boys wanted to know what had happened, and Tiger told them. When he got through, one of the boys said, "Why didn't you just step off the jughead, Tiger, and come on to the house?"

Tiger's face took on a look of startled amazement. "Come to the house!" he exclaimed. "Why, hell's fire, man! The house was four mile off! Expect me to *walk* that far?"

Today, Tiger is still breaking horses for West Texas ranchers, like always; but it's been several years now since he threw the fight to the whiskey bottle and swore off for good.

When that startling event took place, the news rocked the whole West Texas ranch country. Some folks couldn't believe it, and those who did were at a complete loss to explain such a phenomenon. But the explanation, when Tiger finally got around to giving it to Fat, sounded logical enough—at least to Tiger.

"It was like this," he said gravely. "I happened to get caught sober among a bunch of drunks one day, and I haven't been able to look down the neck of a bottle since."

12

THE West Texas cow country had its full quota of characters, like Tiger, and as Fat moved from one ranch to another, he got acquainted with many of them.

One was a cowhand we'll call Jake, who rode for the Elsinore Cattle Company. Jake was long and lanky, a little tongue-tied, and not any smarter than he needed to be. Jake liked to think of himself as a high-rolling bronc-buster, and if somebody inferred that he couldn't ride a particular horse, that was the horse Jake was bound to try. Generally, the horse made a windmill out of him, and it seemed like the only way Jake could land was flat on his back. When he hit, it sounded like somebody had smacked a wet rope against the ground.

When he finally managed to get up and start staggering around, somebody would always ask him if he aimed to make another try, and Jake would always shake his head and give the same answer. "Wa-wasn't for my m-m-mother, I'd r-r-ride him. But I'm all the b-b-boy she's got, and she'd h-h-hate to see me g-g-get hurt."

He came up with that answer so often that it got to be a standing joke among the Elsinore cowhands. Any time one of them drew a horse that he couldn't ride, he'd say, "If it wasn't for my mother, I'd ride him!"

Jake got off from work for a few days one time and made a trip to El Paso, and before he could get out, he'd married a woman we'll call Elvira. And while Elvira wasn't the prettiest or the freshest-looking flower of the desert, she seemed to suit Jake fine. He brought her back, mighty proud of his conquest, and took her to live out in the cow camp, the only home he had.

During the day, while Jake was out with the roundup crew, Elvira would hang around camp, sipping coffee and sampling the cook's grub and taking long siestas in the shade of the wagon. Then, when the day's work was over, here would come Jake, riding in to eat a quick supper before dragging his bedroll off the wagon and calling Elvira to come along. The two of them would bed down for a night of love-making, far enough from the campfire to be out of sight, but seldom out of hearing.

The rest of the cowhands would squat around the fire on their boot heels, listening to Jake and Elvira, grinning at each other and making comments on how well Jake was holding up under the strain of riding herd all day and making love all night.

For a couple of weeks there, Jake's and Elvira's love burned as hot and fierce as a fire in dry grass. But finally it began to burn out. The two of them took to quarreling, and they went at it every night just as loudly and fiercely as they had formerly loved.

Of course, the cowhands listening in couldn't keep out of the quarrel. Some sided with Jake and some backed Elvira, offering every sort of suggestion to help her win the argument.

One night, while the two lay in their bedroll, quarreling away, Jake suddenly shouted, "D-d-dammit to hell! You don't have to sleep in this old b-b-bed!"

Fat, who was lying off out in the dark listening in, raised up and said with true gallantry, "If you don't want to sleep in his old bed, Elvira, you're welcome to sleep in mine."

And that's exactly what Elvira did.

Fat could wish a thousand times that he'd kept his big mouth shut, but Elvira came and crawled into his bedroll, which, out in the dark like that, might not have been so bad if it hadn't been for the rest of the whooping and yelling cowhands.

Fat couldn't get any sleep that night, and they pestered him all the next day; and, for months after Elvira had gone back to El Paso, they were still raw-hiding him about sleeping with a man's wife while the man lay right out there in listening distance.

Fat doesn't guess he'll ever live that one down.

The laziest cowhand Fat ever tried to work with is one he called Sleepy. Sleepy would get out and hustle hard—when the boss was around. But quick as Sleepy thought he was safe, he could sure do a prime job of round-siding in the shade.

Sleepy finally got cured, however, and Fat was there when it happened.

This took place on the Julian Bassett Block Y outfit near Dryden. The boss had to be gone for the day; so he sent Sleepy and Fat and a high-strung, hotheaded young cowhand called Jess to pen a bunch of cattle at a water trap in the far side of the ranch.

Since the work was going to last a good while, they took along a wagon to haul their camping plunder. They'd just reached the windmill and were getting camp set up when Jess spied a bunch of cattle not far out on the range. He suggested that it might save them some hard hunting later on if they penned that bunch right now.

So he and Fat saddled up, and Sleepy told them to go ahead, he'd be along as soon as he put some new lacing in his stirrup leathers.

It was rough country there for cow running. Big flat-topped rocks lying on the surface of the ground, slick as grease under the shoes of a running horse. Tall ocotillo, with their thorny limbs crooked just right to reach out and claw a hunk of meat out of a man's arm or leg. Rock-benched slopes dropping off into steep gullies.

And the cattle turned out to be a spooky bunch that'd drive pretty well till they got in sight of the pens where the trap gate stood open; then they'd snort and light out for the far places with their tails in the air.

Fat and Jess went at it hard and fast. They'd get the cattle bunched and headed in the right direction, only to lose them every time they got in sight of the trap. This happened again and again, until it was plain to both riders that if they ever aimed to pen the cattle, they'd have to have help.

Finally, when their horses had just about gone their limit and Jess's patience was 'way past it, Jess set his horse down beside Fat and said, "Now where'n the hell you reckon that Sleepy's got off to?"

Fat, who knew Sleepy better than Jess did, said, "Well, my guess'd be that he's a-laying up yonder under that wagon asleep."

Jess stared at Fat for a second, while his face got red and his eyes bulged out; then he wheeled his horse and went galloping toward the wagon. Sure enough, just as Fat had predicted, there lay Sleepy, dead to the world. He was sprawled on his saddle blanket, with his saddle for a pillow and his crossed feet propped up on a rock, the most comfortable and blissfully happy-looking cowboy who ever snored in the shade of a wagon.

The sight of such comfort was more than the worn-out Jess could stand. He reached for his rope and dropped his loop over Sleepy's protruding feet, then wheeled his horse and set the spurs to him. And out through the rocks and sotol and cactus and ocotillo they went, with Sleepy dragging at the end of that rope and squawling his head off while Jess cussed him for a full hundred yards before finally sliding his horse to a halt.

"Now, you sorry no-account deadhead," Jess wound up, as he gave Sleepy some rope slack, "you git up and git on the job. You draw the same wages as we do, and from now on, while I'm around, you'll do the same amount of work!"

From the way Sleepy was skinned up and bristling all over with pear spines, Fat didn't think the cowhand could even climb on a horse, much less make a hand. But he was mistaken. It wasn't five minutes before Sleepy had him a horse saddled and was on the job, out-riding Fat and Jess both in his efforts to pen them spooky cattle.

Howard Capps, who roped the sheep in mid-air, was a sandy-headed cowhand from Melvin, Texas, with a habit of getting off alone somewhere and holding conversations with himself.

Fat got a chance to listen in on one of these little

89

personal talks of Howard's one day while the two were trying to round up some heifers along the Pecos River.

Fat will admit that the work they had to do was enough to make a man talk to himself. These heifers were as flighty and fractious as a bunch of sixteen-year-old schoolgirls. Jump a bunch, and they'd scatter like flushed quail. And what with the sun bearing down, blistering hot, and the alkali dust boiling up to sear a man's eyeballs, neither horses nor riders were getting any great lot of fun out of chasing those heifers through the thick stands of thorny quick-growth mesquite.

In the chase, Fat and Howard got split up for a while. Some thirty minutes later, Fat topped out a rise, then pulled his horse to a sudden halt.

Below him was a deep swag, filled with mesquite brush so thick and tangled a man couldn't have stirred them with a pitchfork. At the edge sat Howard on his horse, having a man-to-man talk with himself.

"All right, Mr. Capps," Howard was saying angrily. "Your folks wanted to give you an education. Begged you to go to school where you'd learn how to make an easy living. But hell, no; you had to be smart. You had to be a cowhand.

"So now you're a cowhand, Mr. Capps. A double-tough, hard-riding, hell-raising cowhand. And yonder in that thicket is a bunch of heifers it'll take that sort of cowhand to get out. So just bow your neck and go in after 'em. You asked for it!"

Fat sat, grinning, while Howard bowed his neck and hooked spurs to his sweat-lathered horse; and horse and rider plunged through thorny mesquites and came out on the far side with Howard's shirt hanging in strings, his hat gone, and his face bloody.

But Howard had brought the heifers out ahead of him, just like the hard-riding, double-tough, hell-raising cowhand he'd set out to be.

13

ANYBODY poking around in the God-lost desert mountains of the Texas Big Bend can readily understand why the Indians named them the Chisos or "Ghost" Mountains.

Let come a night of full moon when the deep canyons are black as the inside of a grave and the peaks stick up in the moonlight like the bared fangs of some prehistoric monster, and a man doesn't need a lot of imagination to feel the ghosts of the Old Ones breathing cold down the back of his neck.

At least, that's the way Fat felt about those mountains the first time he ever rode into them. And, as luck would have it, he found himself a ghost in there, too.

He was horse hunting at the time, having been hired by W. S. Warren to help locate and catch out some saddle horses that had strayed off the home range and thrown in with a bunch of wild mares ranging up in the Chisos. He went in with two boys named Charlie and Dep, who knew the country. They drove before them a little bunch of gentle saddle horses to be used as hold-ups for the wild ones and a couple of pack mules to carry their camping plunder.

It was the sort of trip that Fat always looked forward to making—new country to see and a chance for lots of action and excitement.

It was late afternoon when they finally rode up into the forest of pine and weeping juniper, and jumped a little band of fantails. These are a small native deer, smaller even than the common whitetail, yet so fierce that they can rout any big blacktail that grazes up into the high places they claim as their own.

About that time, Charlie looked off down a long slant and sighted four or five miles away what looked to him like a band of wild horses. He told Fat to take the pack mules and loose horses down into the bowl-shaped valley ahead of them and make camp, while he and Dep took a ride down that slant. He said there was water down there, and Fat could locate it by an old jacal, or brush shack, that some Mexican had thrown up in times past.

So Charlie and Dep rode off, and Fat put his horses down a slant so sharp they were nearly walking on their heads.

Out in front of him the sun was setting in the western gap of the mountains known as the Big Window, and about him the shadows lay black and long on the slopes.

He found the water, like Charlie had said, by locating the little jacal. But the shack stood in the black shadow of a high peak and looked sort of spooky to Fat, and, since the water hole was off from it a piece, he stayed away from the shack and pitched camp out in the open.

He stripped the gear from his mount, unloaded the pack mules, and hobbled the animals out to graze. Then he went about building a fire and rustling supper.

The sun sank out of sight. Supper was done, warmed over, and now cold again; still Fat's partners didn't

93

show up. Night came on. The first light of a rising moon touched Casa Grande Peak with glowing silver. The moon climbed higher, shooting long banners of soft light between the jagged peaks, leaving stretches of black shadows in between.

By now, the horses and pack mules had grazed out of hearing and the night quiet had settled down. Off yonder on a high rise a wolf howled. Down in some deep canyon a night owl started booming. A prowling panther squalled like a scared woman. A little night breeze pulled across the bowl and it had a cold edge to it. Fat felt a shiver run through him.

All this was natural, the sort of thing a man could expect, out in the open like this. But knowing this fact still didn't keep Fat from feeling mighty alone. He sure wished his horse-hunting partners would ride in.

Along about then is when he first heard his ghost. It was prowling around the abandoned jacal; and the first time Fat heard the low, grunting moan it made, he wasn't right sure he'd heard anything. Still, he felt a little cold chill crawl up the crease of his backbone. He bent a careful ear in the direction of the shack, and the next time the sound came, he felt his scalp shifting under his hat.

Fat started to his feet—then suddenly laughed. Hell, that couldn't be anything except a complaining wind in one of the canyons. He sat back down by the fire.

Almost at once, he was back on his feet. This time, the moan was louder and punctuated by strained, coughing grunts. There was no getting around it—there was something down there around that brush shack, something that sounded pretty awful.

94

Fat turned and threw a big chunk of wood on the fire, starting a high blaze to help shove back the night. By now, the moon was up and flooding the valley with light nearly as bright as day, but Fat still felt the need of more light.

The flames leaped up. The fire crackled and roared. But none of that shut out that ghostly sound coming from the jacal. The moans and straining grunts rose higher, with now and then a sort of rasping sigh that was as hard on Fat's nerves as the scratching sound of fingernails against a rusty tin bucket.

Up to this time, Fat never had taken much stock in ghosts and spooks and haunted houses and such. But now, he wasn't right sure. His mind got to lunging around and finally broke halter, and he started recollecting all the wild tales he'd ever heard come out of the Chisos.

There was the tale of those old Spanish priests who, back a couple or three hundred years ago, used to work a gold mine in the mountains here with Indian slaves. Then, suddenly, priests, slaves, gold mine and all disappeared, leaving only the clanking of the slaves' leg irons that some said could still be heard here of a stormy night.

There was that Mexican girl who followed a lost lover into the Chisos, hunting him till she died, and the border Mexicans all claimed you could still sometimes hear her anguished callings from the deep canyons.

Then there was Bill Kelly, a Seminole Indian, who discovered what was reckoned to be the Lost Nigger mine, but who disappeared the day after the chunk of quartz he'd brought in was assayed to run $85,000 to the ton.

Following clues left by Kelly, four men searched for and claimed discovery of the mine, only to meet with violent deaths before they got a chance to return. One of these men was Will Stilwell, whose brother Roy still lived at Alpine.

What happened to all those people? Was there some awful spirit or ghost haunting the Chisos and resenting all trespassers?

In broad-open daylight, Fat would have laughed at the idea; but now, he wasn't so sure. He sat huddled up to his fire, so close that he was scorching his backside, and listened to those terrible moans, and shivered, and wished his partners would ride in, and kept wondering about ghosts in general, till it finally came to him that he was acting a complete fool.

Whatever made those sounds down yonder had to be something natural, and he told himself that the smart thing to do was go find out what it was before his imagination scared him to death.

He dug around through the packs till he located a .45 six-shooter and a rusty hatchet with gaps in the blade. Armed with these, he marched bravely off down the slant toward the shack. But he soon learned that telling himself to go investigate that shack was one thing; making himself do it was something else.

Before he'd gone fifty yards, a great sobbing moan rose out of the hut; and, the next thing Fat knew, he was back at the fire.

He sat there awhile, ashamed of himself and remembering a piece of advice his grandpa used to give him.

His grandpa always said, "There ain't nothing wrong with running; but don't ever run till you know what you're running from." It had always sounded like good advice to Fat, but now he got to wondering what his grandpa would have done in a case like this. And, finally, he decided that his grandpa would have gone down there and found out what was making that noise. So Fat braced himself and tried it again. And failed again.

Fat is ashamed to admit how many times he repeated this act. Twice, he got right up to the door. Both times a sudden stroke of heart failure hit him and he had to run back to the fire to warm up his courage.

Once he stumped his toe and fell down and pulled off his six-shooter, and the shot aroused echoes that must have been asleep for a thousand years, judging from the way the mountainsides shot back at him.

Fat declares that, by this time, if it hadn't been for the other horse hunters, he would have called off his ghost hunt, broken camp, and quit the mountains. But he couldn't afford to leave his partners, and also he couldn't afford to sit by the fire and wait till they came in. They'd hear the sounds and want to know what made them; and if Fat said he hadn't been to see, it wouldn't take a lot of brainwork for them to figure out why. So, quick as he could get a nose-twist on his nerve, he went back down to the shack.

This time, Fat carried a third weapon, the dead clump of a sotol to which the bloom stalk was still attached. He set fire to the oily blades and carried it poked out ahead of him. Any ghost that made a run at him was sure going to get its feathers scorched.

97

Armed with his flaming brand, Fat stepped up to the door of the shack. His heart was flopping against his ribs like a catfish in a sack, and his hair was pushing up his hat; nevertheless, he'd made up his mind to go all the way this time.

Just then he heard a scuffling sound inside the shack. Sobbing, choking moans seemed to come up from all around him. Fat's blood turned to ice water. With a yell, he flung the burning sotol through the door and wheeled to run—only to cross his spur shanks and fall.

He hit hard, but instantly rolled up to a sitting position. He took a wild glance over his shoulder. There, inside the shack, the burning sotol lay on the packed-dirt floor, casting a wavery light on the brush walls.

And against the far side Fat saw the convulsive movement of some formless creature rising right up out of the earth itself.

Fat didn't even try to get to his feet. He doubts that his rubbery legs would have held him if he had. He sat right where he was and emptied the six-shooter into the thing before it could rise up and come to get him.

The gunfire cracked against the mountain walls with whiplash reports and rolled loud and heavy in the canyons. But when the echoes finally died away, there wasn't a sound left besides the crackle of the burning sotol. No moans, no movement of any sort.

Fat got to his feet. He reckoned he'd sure settled that ghost's hash for good. But when he entered the shack for a look, he had his empty six-shooter clubbed and was holding his broken-bladed hatchet drawn back and ready.

What he found was sure a letdown for a ghost-killer.

It was a scrubby calf that had been eating sotol and had gotten the cabbage-like head lodged in its throat.

The poor creature had been slowly choking to death, but it was out of its misery now. Fat hadn't missed it with a single shot.

Fat was back at the campfire, all done with his scare, and laughing at himself for being such a fool, when, right at his elbow, somebody hollered, "Is supper ready?"

Fat jumped clear over the fire before it came to him that his partners had finally ridden in.

Fat says they stayed up there in the mountains for a couple of weeks and must have caught some of the horses they went after, but any time he tries to think back to that first trip to the Chisos, all he can really recollect is the ghost he stalked and killed in there.

14

THE screen, song, and fiction version of "Old Paint," the traditional cow horse, and his traditional gun-slinging, rope-twirling, guitar-picking cowboy master will probably live as long as there's even a legend of the American cowboy left. Their relationship is so beautiful, their devotion to each other so singular and heart-warming, that the chances are they'll move right on down through time, lovingly saving each other's lives several times a day and all but eating out of the same feedbag.

And it's probably just as well that such a sweet story does live on. If a whole rodeo audience can be moved to tears by the show act of faithful Old Paint's returning in the face of flying bullets to stand guard over the body of his dying master—well, nobody yet has ever disproved the value of tears as an emotional release.

On top of that, as Fat points out, there's really nothing wrong with the story, other than its having so little foundation in fact. It definitely couldn't have come out of the relationship between a working cowboy and a working cow horse.

To begin with, riders on every cow range in the West hold a standing grudge against paint horses. Give them their pick of a *remuda,* and they invariably choose horses with solid coloring. Paints, glass-eyes, and off-colored duns are generally considered too high-strung and fractious. Get in a tight with one, and he's likely to lose his head and fall to pieces.

But more important is the fact that cow horses are freedom-loving creatures who, as any horsebreaker will tell you, had a lot rather kill a man than submit to slavery.

Which isn't to say no cow horse can be trusted. Handled right, even a high-spirited horse can be gentled till he's not fighting back every chance he gets. He can be taught to do his work and even take pride in it.

The big trouble, however, is that it takes time to train an animal in any such manner, and, out on the big ranches of the West, there's seldom that much time to spend on a horse.

The working cowhand sure can't do it. He's too busy rounding up cattle, roping them and branding them and doctoring them for screw worms. And if the horse he draws to do his work on happens to have leanings toward manslaughter, that's an added difficulty but it doesn't change the situation any. The boss is paying the cowhand wages for getting the cow work done, not for spending the weeks and months necessary for making a devoted pal out of "Old Paint."

So, of course, any time a drifting cowhand comes across a "good" cow horse, he's as surprised and delighted as a kid handed a sack of candy by a total stranger.

In all his years of cow work, Fat can recollect only one such horse. And the ironic fact is that this horse was called "Old Paint."

Fat first came across the paint in the *remuda* of the

101

Todd NH outfit, operating in Crockett County. He rode him for only a few days that time, but came to the same conclusion about him as Earl Salmon had: Old Paint was a working cowhand's "dream horse." And ever afterward, although Fat and Earl were the best of friends, any time they rode for the Todd outfit at the same time, they fell out with each other over who was to ride Old Paint.

Paint wasn't much for looks. He stood too tall, better than fifteen hands high, and always looked worn out and half starved. But, once under a saddle, he could be depended on. A rider could be running the devil out of a wild horse but still needing a little extra speed, and Paint always had some in reserve. Jump a cow in the roughest country, and Paint would put a roper up within reach. Let a bunch of cows or sheep start milling, and Paint could break up the mill faster than a man. A rider didn't even have to pick up his reins. Just let Paint go; he'd move in, take hold, and get the job done.

A cowhand, used to having to work on any and every thing that even resembles a horse, comes to appreciate and respect an animal like Paint. And while Paint didn't ever seem particularly concerned about whether or not anybody appreciated him, he sure saw to it that he was accorded respect. He was able and willing to do his work and he did it without any fuss and bother. But let a new rider get to pranking on him or try to put him in some place where he had more sense than to go, and Paint could sure set that cowboy straight in a hurry about who was running the show. He could stack a rider on the ground as neat and solid as a cord of stovewood. And that went for the best riders in the country. Some might stay in the saddle longer than others, but when Paint bogged his head and really went after it, he could put any rider to picking daisies.

He'd been that way from the start. He was born on the Blackstone & Slaughter ranch on the Pecos, out of the Berry Ketchum stock of horses. And while he was still a colt, somebody gave him to Lee Perkins, who was then bossing the NH outfit. Lee tried to get him broken but didn't have a rider on the place who could handle him. Paint threw and bit and kicked and ran over Perkins' riders till half the crew was crippling around; so Perkins finally turned him over to Abe Caruthers, a bronc-peeler for the Montagues.

Well, Abe didn't have much better luck with Paint than the rest. Sometimes he could ride him—or Paint let him ride—and other times he couldn't. But Abe soon learned one thing—any time he could stay in the saddle, he sure had a horse between his legs. Get Old Paint out of the notion of pitching, and he could catch any wild jack running loose in the country. Fastest thing afoot, Abe told Mark Taliaferro. And Mark, after riding Paint in a wild-jack chase or two, agreed. And that's when they decided to make a race horse out of him.

They took him in to Ozona, where they shod him and curried and combed him and fed him oats till his hair shone. They exercised him when they could stay on him, getting him all trimmed up and ready for the big Fourth of July rodeo and races.

The only thing was, neither Mark nor Abe wanted to ride Paint in that race. So they got to looking around

103

and finally decided the jockey they needed was a Negro man working for Abe.

The Negro had noticed Paint's habit of jerking loose from a rider any time he took a notion and wasn't too sure he wanted the job. His wife, who cooked for Abe, was certain he didn't. She told her man he was liable to get killed, fooling with that Paint horse, and she probably would have kept him from it if Abe and Mark hadn't kept priming their rider's courage with tequila.

They'd buy the Negro a bottle, and as long as it lasted he had plenty of confidence in himself and the manly courage to keep his complaining wife hushed up. But as soon as the bottle went dry and the glow faded, the Negro would start having doubts, and his wife was no longer afraid to give him hell again. So Mark and Abe would have to go off and buy another bottle of tequila.

They'd each spent something like twenty dollars on tequila by the time the day of the races came around. However, they had the Negro jockey, slightly glassy-eyed but confident, sitting astride Paint when they led the horse up to the starting post. Which was enough for Mark and Abe. They knew they had a winning horse out there. They hurried through the crowd, making all the last-minute bets they could get.

They had another man out on the track, holding Paint out on the ends of the reins, just to make certain he didn't start anything. After all, he was just a country horse, and this noise and excitement were new to him.

But that wasn't necessary. Paint stood right in line beside all the town horses, and never blinked an eye till the bell rang. Then he left out like a glory-bound bat.

There were seven or eight horses in that race, some of them good ones. There was that Walter Kay horse from Pontotoc, a beauty on any man's race track. She'd been winning all over the country, and that's how come Mark and Abe could get such good odds, betting on Old Paint. But the racers hadn't run more than two hundred yards till Old Paint was fifty yards in the lead and still pulling ahead. And hunched over his neck was Abe's Negro, loaded to the gills on tequila, but handling his horse with all the grace and skill of an experienced jockey. Riding for a win and the big money.

The crowd went wild. Abe and Mark were jumping up and down, waving their fists and yelling with triumph.

Then, right there within a hundred yards of the finish line, so far ahead that the other jockeys couldn't have shot him with a .30–.30, Paint, for no reason anybody ever figured out, suddenly broke stride, tucked both head and tail, and threw his rider so high it looked like he turned over twice before he hit the ground. That done, he galloped to the rail, leaped it like a deer, and went calmly about grazing in the tall green grass of the pasture on the other side.

Well, of course, people ran out to rescue the Negro, who lay in the middle of the track; but they couldn't get there quick enough. Here came the rest of the hard-running racers. And, while it was certain that some of the ponies jumped his body, they kicked up such a fog of dust doing it that nobody could be sure that all did.

When people finally did get to the black man, he was lying there so sprawled out and limp he had to be dead.

The people stood back and looked at each other and

shook their heads and wished they knew something to do and did nothing. Finally the Negro's wife came charging through them to grab her man by the shirt collar and shake him.

"Git up from there, you low-lifing black man!" she ordered. "Don't I keep telling you this pore white trash is fixing to git you killed?"

Which seemed to be all the Negro needed to put some starch back into his bones. He looked meek and dejected enough to have stood a good bracer of tequila if Mark and Abe had had the bottle along, but he didn't stagger or reel as he followed his woman off the track.

Well, of course, after losing Mark and Abe that much money, Paint had ruined any chance he might have had for glory on the race track. Abe got him out of town as quick as he could and turned him over to a horsebreaker by the name of Cayetaño Vascas, with orders to break or kill him, just whichever suited him.

Cayetaño chose to break him. The Mexican had a knack with horses that few men could equal, and he did a much better job of making a cow horse of Old Paint than anybody else ever had. He might have gentled him completely if it hadn't been for a black jenny running wild in the west side of the Montague ranch. This jenny kept luring off gentle cow horses to run wild with her, and every horse owner in the country was wanting to rope her and get rid of her, and a lot of them had tried; but nobody had a horse fast and long-winded enough to run her down.

Well, the subject of this wild jenny came up again one day, and Cayetaño said that if they wanted her caught he had the horse to catch her on. They told him to have at it, and Cayetaño did.

Abe Caruthers heard about the hunt and rode with Cayetaño. They jumped the black jenny back in the cedar brakes, and the Mexican rider got a good run at her down a long sharp slant. Old Paint, he had his ears laid back and was coming down that rocky slope like a runaway train, walking right up on that fast-footed jenny. And Cayetaño was reaching for his catch-rope when the jenny came to a stretch of barbwire fence that Cayetaño hadn't known was being built. The jenny leaped the fence, but Old Paint didn't see it in time.

Abe Caruthers was a quarter of a mile behind in the chase when he heard Old Paint hit that tight-strung fence. He spurred on, full of the sickening conviction that Cayetaño and Old Paint would both be dead when he got there. And Cayetaño nearly was. He and Old Paint were both over the fence. Cayetaño lay on the ground, knocked cold, while Old Paint stood off to one side, snorting at the blood that both were spilling on the ground.

Cayetaño stayed unconscious for four days, and when he came to he wasn't in any fit shape to ride Paint or any other horse for a good long spell.

So Paint, whose cuts had been superficial, was turned over to a wolf hunter; and he proved to be the sort of horse that man was looking for. Following a fast-running pack of wolf hounds was just about the sort of job Paint needed. Those long fast runs took a little of the keenness off the edge of Paint's temper. After an all-night run on the heels of that high-singing pack, Paint wasn't quite so quick to fall to pieces every time the least little thing didn't suit him. Or it could have been that he got as big a thrill out of those wolf chases as the hounds did. The wolf hunter said it wasn't any time till

107

Paint was listening as hard as he was for a hound to open on a trail. And the instant he heard the sound, he'd start quivering all over and fighting the bits to get his head. Turn him loose then, and he'd still be stacking the landscape behind him when daylight came.

He'd come in plenty jaded, looking as thin and gaunt as a gutted snowbird. But when night came, the wolf hunter could set his rig on him and turn loose the hounds, and Paint would be ready to go again.

That sort of life was enough to kill off most horses within a few years, but it didn't kill Paint. When his wolf-running days ended, he was put to running cattle. He did a good job of it, too, under any cowhand who had an understanding of horses and treated him right. But, like a lot of cowhands, he drifted from one ranch to another, being traded off generally on account of having piled too many riders.

He got old and then he got older, but it didn't seem to make any difference. He was still a good hard-working cow horse, with plenty of pride and the ability to make any cowhand respect him.

The last time Fat and Earl Salmon quarreled over who was to get him in his string, Paint was twenty-five years old; and Fat, who won him that time, was careful to keep a tight hold on what he called the "Whoa reins."

"Me'n Paint, we was both gray-headed by then," Fat said, "but damned if I don't believe he was the friskiest one of the two. I wasn't taking no chances on letting him get his head down!"

15

THERE during the twenties, a lot of working cow-hands, like Fat's friend Mac, began to forsake the horse for an automobile. Not for doing their cow work, of course, but as a means of transportation from one job to another.

The older cowhands, more set in their ways, didn't hold with any such outlandish change. A good piece of horseflesh had always been good enough for them, and they argued that a real cowhand had too much pride to go clattering and bouncing across the range in one of them stinking automobile machines.

But the young are always more subject to change; so the young riders argued right back. They pointed out that a man with a car could get around from one job to another quicker than a man on a horse; he could range wider and pick up more jobs. A car would save the cost of keeping and feeding a mount between jobs, too. A man with a car could haul his saddle gear around with him and ride the other man's horse. Then, too, a car gave him a better chance to run into town of a night after quitting time, in case he wasn't caught up on his courting. And what young cowhand ever was?

Fat was still young enough to get the fever. He saved up enough money to buy himself a Model T. At first, he couldn't do much more than sort of loose-herd it down a road. Sometimes he couldn't even keep it there. But there was always plenty of room on either side of the road, and generally the barbwire fences needed tearing down and rebuilding before he ever went through them, anyhow.

But it wasn't long before he got the hang of driving and could pin the gas and spark levers back like the ears of a fast-running jack rabbit and go rattling off in a fog of alkali, faster than any jack rabbit ever hoped to travel.

He was working out of Ozona at the time he bought his car, riding partners with a young cowhand who was panting around a couple of girls in town. These girls were so sweet and pretty, Fat's partner couldn't make up his mind which one he was after.

The only trouble was, this partner had no car. Said he was saving up for one but didn't have it yet. He couldn't get to go see the girls often, and he was scared to death that some of the town boys would cut in on him. He asked Fat why didn't he throw in with him. Said, with a car like Fat's to take the girls riding in, the two of them would be a cinch to keep them town boys stood off.

Fat considered. He wasn't one of these tall, dark, handsome birds who buckle the knees of every young female that laid an eye on him. Still, he wore pants; and he'd noticed what a surprising number of women didn't ask any more of a man. And driving up in his own car like that . . .

These girls were sisters and just as pretty and sweet-natured as Fat's partner claimed they were. Before Fat quite realized it, he was spending half his wages on gasoline to take those girls riding and to buy them

110

candy and soft drinks. And he was out so much every night that he wasn't getting sleep enough to keep a cat alive.

Worse than that, even, he was getting ideas. Girls like those sisters—a man wouldn't be ashamed to take home and show off to his mama. In fact, he'd be about half proud for his mama to know that he could go with such fine girls.

From that, Fat got to figuring how he could save a lot more of his wages if he tried, and how soon those wages might add up to enough for two people to live on.

It was a real pretty dream, but, like most such dreams, it soon faded to nothing in the face of reality.

There came a night when Fat was tied up with ranch work and couldn't get away. He loaned his Model T to his saddle partner, and it was long after sunup the next morning when the great lover came in, looking popeyed enough to have been shot at and missed.

Which, Fat soon learned, was exactly what had happened. His partner and one of the girls had gone out driving, and the Model T engine had taken a cranky spell and quit on them. They'd had to work on it all night, trying to get it started again. Day was breaking when they finally drove up to the front-yard gate. And there stood Papa in the front door, waiting for them.

Papa was a good, religious sort of old man, a preacher by trade, who wouldn't stand for any wild young cowhand's keeping his daughter out all night, ruining her reputation and no telling what all else. He upped with a shotgun and opened some rain holes in the cloth top of Fat's Model T. And Fat's partner was convinced that

111

if he hadn't already had that Model T eared back to the last notch of speed when the gun went off, he'd right that minute be a dead cowboy in the streets of Ozona.

Well, that fixed things. The girl Fat had been taking out, she was sure sweet and nice. But with a Papa like that . . .!

Sometimes now, Fat gets to thinking that maybe he ought to have gone ahead and taken the risk. She sure was a sweet little girl. But then, he gets to looking around at other cowhands who married little things just as sweet, and he sort of pities them. These old boys must find it a terrible surprise and disappointment to learn how fast that sweetness can sour out, once a woman's got a man roped and tied.

With a car, Fat was now able to visit his folks more often. And what always surprised him at each visit was the changes taking place in the family.

He'd come in, thinking of his folks like they'd been the last time he'd seen them, only to find everything different. Once he visited home to find that Cumine, his younger sister next to him, had married and moved 'way off to Michigan. And a baby had been born and named Cynthia. Fat scoffed at that name, told the family that the poor little thing never would get its proper growth with a name like that. "Bessie, now," he told them. "That's a good, plain name. A girl might have a chance with a name like that."

So the next time he was home, the family had named the latest girl-child Bessie, and, sure enough, Cynthia was little and frail, much too small for her age.

Seemed like Fat was always finding a new baby at home; or one of the younger children who'd just been a baby the last trip home would now suddenly be a foot taller. One year, there in 1927, three of the kids married. Benny had started it off in April. Then the love bug got in a deep bite on old slow-going bachelor Larence, and he married in June. And, in November, Otis up and married.

After learning of all that marrying, Fat wasn't surprised when his mother called him off for a private talk one day and demanded to know when he was going to marry some nice girl and settle down.

"Now, Mama," he grinned at her. "You know no girl's going to fall in love with an old boy like me, with a face as ugly as hammered mud."

The real truth was that Fat didn't see anything particularly wrong with leading a single life. Sometimes, he might sort of wish he had a wife, but when he took notice of what happened to a lot of men who had wives, he wasn't so sure that matrimony was the most blissful state of existence. The way he came to look at it, a single man got lonesome at times, but he sure had a lot less troubles and worries to put up with.

Now when he went home, there never seemed to be much change in his mother. She was getting maybe just a little heavier than she'd once been, but there wasn't even a hint of gray in her hair. How she could stand up to bearing and rearing the family she had and still remain little and quick-moving and cheerful and pretty as ever was always a marvel to Fat.

Julius Alford, though, wasn't holding up so well. There was plenty of gray in his hair. And, although he still worked, as always, it seemed to Fat that his father didn't have the push and go he'd once had. Once the old man had had a big booming laugh that seemed to come all the way up from his heels. Now, Fat had to think up ways to bring that laugh out again.

One time when Fat arrived home in the middle of the night, his mother got up to light a lamp and show him his new sister, Dolorece. The old man got up out of his bed in another room and came in, and Fat started in to hooraw him a little, telling him that he was real proud of him, that he'd thought a man of fifty-six was too old to father another baby.

None of the other children ever dared joke with the old man now like Fat did, but Fat could generally get by with it. And on this night, Julius Alford seemed grateful to have somebody to pick at him a little and finally invited his son to come sleep in the same bed with him.

So they got into bed, and the companionable talk drifted from one thing to another till finally the old man got off on the subject of chicken snakes. He said this was the worst year for chicken snakes he'd ever seen, that they were all over the place and eating up every baby chicken his wife could hatch off. Then he told a chicken-snake yarn or two, and Fat added a couple of his own, and finally the talk ran out and they'd just about dropped off to sleep when they heard a rustling noise against a shovel standing in the nearby fireplace.

Instantly, the old man sat up in bed. "Why, that's one of them chicken snakes now!" he yelped.

He fumbled around on the floor for his flashlight, found it, and pressed the button. He swung the beam of light into the fireplace, and, sure enough, right there behind the shovel were the splotched-back coils of a chicken snake.

Fat watched comfortably from the bed while his father got up and stomped around the room in his bare feet, hunting the misplaced poker with which to kill the snake. But by the time he'd found the poker and come back, the snake had disappeared into some of the rock crevices of the fireplace, and Julius Alford couldn't seem to find it.

He was squatted down in his union-suit drawers, moving his light this way and that, when Fat reached for the broom that stood in the corner close at hand. Taking care to make no sound, Fat lifted the broom over the old man's bare feet and dragged it gently back across them.

"Damnation!" the old man exploded, and it seemed to Fat that his father ran halfway up the wall to the ceiling before he let the poker clatter to the floor and dropped back and stumbled over it as he tried to escape.

When he caught onto what had happened, Julius Alford grabbed up the poker and came at his son with it. But Fat had already rolled out of bed and was now beating it for the door, shouting with laughter.

Fat ran out across the porch and into the yard, where he stood in the dark and listened to the old man daring him to come back inside. He waited till his mother lit the lamp again and helped his father kill the snake; then, when he thought it was safe, he sneaked back onto the porch and went to bed on an empty cot.

He lay there awhile, wondering if maybe he'd been a

115

little rough on the old man, scaring him so; but in a minute he heard his father chuckling to himself. Fat grinned into the darkness and turned over and went to sleep.

16

TOM POWERS of Ozona today ranks among the top five calf ropers of the nation, but there was a time when love of a new saddle came close to spoiling him as a cowhand. He was a kid of about sixteen, working at his first riding job on the Joe Davidson ranch, and, to Tom, there wasn't a thing in the world prettier or more precious than his new saddle.

He all but ate and slept with it. He kept a rag handy to wipe every speck of dust from the shiny new leather. While other cowhands on the ranch stripped their saddles from their mounts and pitched them out on the ground, Tom always hunted for a place to hang his. When a cow he was after took to the tall brush that might scratch the new leather, Tom went to hunting for a way around.

Came a morning when Tom set his rig on a horse he hadn't ridden before. The instant he forked the strange horse, the animal broke in two, blowing up such a storm that Tom couldn't stay with him. First he landed just back of the saddle. Next he went off over the bawling bronc's rump.

Any other cowhand in this unhappy predicament would have called it quits by this time. But not Tom. He was riding with long bridle reins and he kept a firm grip on them while he rode the outlaw's hocks for

117

several jumps. Kicked loose at last, he landed in the dirt where he still kept that fierce grip on his reins, while the horse pitched and stomped all over him.

When it looked like the young cowhand was a goner for sure, Fat ran in to grab the reins away from Tom and fight the horse off.

Helping Tom to his feet, Fat said, "Why in the hell didn't you turn them reins loose, Tom, so he could get offen you!"

Tom wiped a smear of blood and dirt from his face and reached for the bridle reins again. "Think I want that old fool to get loose with my new saddle?" he said.

Studying that one over, Fat came to the conclusion that something had to be done about that new saddle before Tom got himself killed. Fat kept on the watch. A few days later, he saw Tom take his new rig off a horse, spread his blanket out on the ground, then lay his saddle on it, taking care that none of the spotless leather touched the dirt.

Fat figured this was his chance. He moved up close to the saddle. The minute Tom's back was turned, Fat grabbed a stirrup and left out in a run, bawling and squealing and pitching like an outlaw horse, dragging Tom's new saddle in the dust and over sharp rocks and through claw-thorn brush.

When he came to a barbwire fence, he jumped it; but the saddle hung there and that's where Fat left it, because by now the long-legged Tom was close on him, yelling curses at him, threatening to kill him if he ever caught him.

Fat kept running till he was out of rock-throwing distance and had to stay out in the hot sun for a couple of hours before the enraged Tom would let him come back into camp. But, like Fat had figured, once the new had been scuffed and scratched off the young cowhand's saddle, Tom was able to forget about it and go on and make the cowhand he'd showed the promise of making at the start.

Such rowdy pranking is a common form of entertainment for working cowhands; and as a pranker, Fat could hold his own with the best of them. He particularly enjoyed deflating a braggart or putting the spur to some cowhand taking advantage of others.

There was this old boy from Ohio that Joe Davidson hired to help out around the ranch. We'll call him Sore Toe, because Fat's forgotten his name, and because for months he kept nursing an ingrown toenail and using it as an excuse to put all the hard work off on somebody else.

Fat first attempted to show up Sore Toe by telling him some lies about the size of the wildcats living in the surrounding cedar hills. These cats, according to Fat, stood as tall as a bull yearling and had so little fear that they'd come right into the house and attack a man in bed. The way he told it, he'd often got up and slammed shut the bunkhouse door just barely in time to keep the big man-eaters from catching him.

With help from the other cowhands, Fat soon had Sore Toe so jittery that he'd hardly crack a door after dark.

Then came a hot night, when all the cowhands slept out on the front gallery of the bunkhouse, hoping to get a breath of air. Sore Toe didn't much want to sleep out

119

there, but was afraid of being laughed at if he didn't; so he finally crippled out with his bedroll, like the rest.

Fat waited till Sore Toe's snores told him that his victim was asleep, then cut loose with a shout. "Wildcats!" he yelled, and emptied a .45 six-shooter into the night.

It got results, all right. It showed that, in spite of that crippling ingrown toenail, Sore Toe was as active as anybody. He quit his bed, running, and tore out through the dark for a hundred yards before he stubbed his toe against a rock, crippling himself so badly this time that the next day he had to be taken to a doctor.

His wildcat fighting having thus backfired till all the other cowhands were laughing at him, Fat was at a loss just what to do about Sore Toe till some days later. He was out at the barn and found Sore Toe climbing painfully up into the loft to pitch down some hay.

Fat said, "Sore Toe, I'll bet you haven't got the nerve to jump out of that loft."

Such a dare touched Sore Toe's pride. "How much'll you bet?" he demanded.

"Why," Fat said, fingering his pocket, "all I've got is a dime, but I'll bet that."

"Well, right here's where you lose that dime," Sore Toe said gleefully, and jumped.

Luck was with Fat. He lost his dime, all right; but the ranch boss happened to step inside the barn in time to see Sore Toe's daring leap and came to the obvious conclusion that anybody who'd jump from that high up didn't have a very sore toe and the thing for Sore Toe to do was to get high behind after some of that work the other cowhands had been doing for him.

120

Howard Capps was as fine a cowboy as Fat ever rode with. Fat liked him a lot, and showed it by pestering the hell out of him. And since Howard had a gunpowder temper and a tendency to cry when he got mad —which shamed him and made him get all the madder—there's been more than one time when their friendship got a little frazzled around the edges.

Take the time they were riding for Wayne West, down on Johnson Draw, south of Ozona. The country had enjoyed a long rainy spell, which brings the green grass but also brings a lot of screw worms. Fat and Howard had a pasture full of screw-worm cases they were having to doctor every day. Finally, here came one of those big gully-humping rains that swelled Johnson Draw out of its banks and kept it flooded for days.

This put Howard and Fat in a bind. The horse trap was on the other side of the draw from camp. They couldn't get across the flood to fresh mounts, and had to go right on roping big cattle on the two horses they had at the time the creek got up. Such heavy work without relief soon had their horses so jaded they could hardly catch a cow, much less hold her.

Finally, the flood went down; Fat and Howard crossed for fresh mounts. But catching fresh horses on muddy ground, while riding mounts so jaded they could hardly lift their feet out of their tracks, called for some figuring.

Fat's horse wasn't quite so far gone as Howard's, so he rode up to the top of the mountain to bring the *remuda* down past Howard, who hoped to get a rope on some horse as they came by.

Well, it worked out pretty well, except for the fact

121

that the first horse to come within roping distance of Howard had only one good eye.

This horse was as gentle as anybody's; he had no call to pull the stunt he did when Howard roped him. The thing was, when the horse came past he had his blind side next to Howard and didn't see him. He wasn't expecting a thing; and when Howard's loop snaked out and settled around his neck, it scared him. He kicked and snorted and tried to jump astraddle of his own neck. Then he left out like a horse that had never had a rope on him.

Howard, not expecting any of this, didn't have his rope tied to his saddle horn; so, of course, the horse jerked it out of his hands.

It was a brand-new rope, a piece of equipment that every cowhand is proud of. But yonder Howard's went, the horse dragging it through the sloppy mud, cutting it with his hind feet every time he stepped on it and frazzling out the fibers as he whipped it through the brush and rocks.

That was enough to make any cowhand mad. But that was only a part of it. In the first place, Howard felt like a fool for not having his rope tied to the saddle horn. In the second place, mounted on a give-out horse, he couldn't do a thing about saving his brand-new rope. In the third place, here came Fat off the side of the mountain with a grin on his face as wide as the wave on a slop bucket.

"By golly, Howard," Fat said. "You afraid to tie your rope to your saddle horn?"

Howard was still young enough to be touchy about his courage. He didn't want anyone to think he was afraid his horse would get jerked down. "Hell, no, I ain't afraid to tie my rope," he told Fat.

"Well, it sure looked like it," Fat said. "I can't see any other reason why you'd let that old horse drag off a new rope through the mud."

Howard didn't answer that one. He swore and gigged his jaded horse off down the slope after the *remuda*.

Fat rode with him a piece, saw by the look on Howard's face how he was hurting, and started baiting him more. He recollected that the only other children in Howard's family were girls, so he said, "Has any of them sisters of yours got any nerve?"

Howard looked around at him. "What do you mean by that?"

"Well, I was just wondering," Fat said. "I noticed that their brother hasn't got no nerve. Just wondered if the girls got it all."

Howard's hot temper had him ready to explode, and this last was too much. He fell out of his saddle and came at Fat.

"Get down off that horse," he raged. "I'll whip you right here!"

Fat moved his horse aside, tickled to death at how mad Howard was. "Why," he said, "if I wasn't afraid I'd hurt you, I'd just get down and give you a good thrashing and maybe learn you something."

Howard's face swelled and started turning purple. "Hurt me!" he raged. "Why, damn you, I'd just like for you to get down here and try it!"

But Fat wouldn't. All he'd do was ride along, keep-

123

ing out of the enraged Howard's way and grinning back over his shoulder at him.

That grin of Fat's, it was so taunting and nasty that Howard couldn't stand it. The tears started and that made him madder than ever. Shouting with rage, he bent down and grabbed up an armful of rocks and started running through the mud, trying to get within throwing distance.

Fat saw now that he'd carried the thing too far. He wasn't afraid of the rocks. There were only three, any one of which was so big that Howard would have had to drop the others to throw it. The thing that had Fat bothered was the possibility that, if he spurred up, Howard might drop his big rocks and pick up some small enough that he could throw.

So Fat rode along at about the same slow pace, and Howard followed doggedly after him, carrying these three big rocks and trying to run in sloppy mud that came nearly to his boot tops, and crying and screaming at Fat and cursing him and begging him to get down off that horse so he could whip him.

Fat rode on, grinning back over his shoulder, but all the time getting a little further ahead till finally, when he figured he had enough lead, he roweled his jaded horse into a stumbling gallop and got away.

He waited about an hour before venturing up to the pen, where Howard had managed to corral the horses. Then he approached warily, ready to turn tail at the first sign of hostilities.

There was a big bunch of rocks piled by the gate, and Howard was standing right beside them. He made no crooked moves, however, merely waited till Fat was

124

up in speaking distance, then said in a disgruntled voice, "Sometimes I think you must have lost your mind."

"Why, Howard," Fat chided, "I don't see how you ever come by that idea."

Howard's good nature got the upper hand, and his mouth twisted up in a one-sided grin. "Damn you," he swore. "Don't you ever make me that mad again."

Fat still gets a big laugh out of how mad he got his friend Howard that day, but there are West Texas cowhands who'll point out that he generally doesn't laugh nearly so loud when Howard's anywhere around.

Sometimes Fat's fool pranking got in the way of the work. When that happened, it didn't make him real popular with the ranch owner.

Clay Adams, sheep rancher and cowboy artist of Ozona, hired Fat and a cowhand by the name of Coon Chandler as extra help for rounding up some fat lambs ready for market. Adams was trying to hurry up the gather, fearing that the trucks coming to haul the lambs would arrive at the ranch before they got the lambs penned and ready. Everything was going fine, however, till Chandler stepped down off his horse for a moment, leaving him standing there with his reins dropped to the ground.

Seeing this, Fat rode up close to the horse and shouted "Whoa!" at the animal.

This, of course, excited the horse, so that it whirled and went trotting off, holding its head sideways to keep from stepping on the reins.

125

Coon started after his horse, shouting at Fat, "What the hell you running my horse off for?"

"Why, I ain't running him off," Fat declared, grinning. "Don't you hear me hollering 'Whoa!' at him?" Then he made a run at the horse, shouting "Whoa!" at him again, scaring him worse than ever.

To a mounted cowhand, there's nothing much more comical than another cowhand trying to chase down a horse afoot. Coon was getting madder by the minute and swearing at the top of his voice at Fat, who was making a big pretense of helping him by rushing up to the horse and hollering "Whoa!" every time Coon reached for the reins.

Everybody quit driving sheep and stopped to watch the show, and by the time Adams had ridden back to see what was causing the delay, Fat had kept Coon and his horse in a trot for a quarter of a mile, while the rest of the riders whooped and shouted with laughter.

"If I'd had a gun right then, I think I'd have shot Fat," Clay Adams says. "Fat'll never know how close he came to getting fired that morning. But, then, I got to thinking how often this same sort of foolishness had kept a crew of overworked cowhands from going sour on me; so I just let it ride.

"When it came to keeping a crew of cowhands in good spirits, I never knew a better man to have on your payroll than Fat Alford."

17

A BIG ranch operator by the name of Reynolds had a bunch of cattle on graze in northern Mexico about a hundred and fifty miles south of Chihuahua City. The cattle market in the States was pretty bad, but worse in Mexico. When the cattle got fat, Reynolds figured he could make money by importing them into Texas. So he sent a picked crew of West Texas cowhands down to help with the roundup, and Fat was one of the bunch.

The hands went down in a Ford pickup, most of them riding atop their saddle gear and camping plunder. They crossed the Rio Grande at Ojinaga and made their headquarters at a huddle of Mexican shacks called Agua Fria, on the banks of a small river by the same name. There, Fat saw the kind of cow country he'd never seen before—or since.

It was rough country, in a way, hilly and pretty rocky underfoot and cut by deep draws and canyons. But none of it was too rough for a good clear-footed horse to travel over; and when it came to grass, a man could hardly believe what he saw. It was grama grass, for the most part, and stood belly deep to a horse in any direction you wanted to ride, even up on the steepest slopes.

There was wild game everywhere—deer, bear, turkey, and quail. Every draw ran clear water. It was the sort of country old-timers claimed that Texas had been before the sod-busting settlers got a whack at it and the ranchers grazed it to the ground, trying to get rich overnight.

It was also a country in which Fat's itchy roping hand got him into a jackpot that only some fast footwork could get him out of.

The thing started when Fat got to noticing a peculiarity of many of the steers they were rounding up. These were mostly all Mexican cattle, varicolored, small in size, but packing plenty of tallow. Fat had seen their kind before and was used to them. What he couldn't understand was the number of bobtailed steers he kept running across. Fully a tenth of the steers were shy of tails.

Fat asked one of the vaqueros named Miguel about it.

"It is the bears, Señor," Miguel explained. "They bite the tails from the cattle and eat them."

Fat looked startled. "But why the tails?" he demanded. "Why don't they just kill the steer and eat it?"

Miguel shrugged. "*Quién sabe,* Señor? Maybe the bear is too small, but it is not impossible that he is too lazy."

Fat didn't know what to believe about such an answer. Could be this Mexican was spoofing him.

But a couple of days later, he learned better. Along about sunset, he and Miguel sighted a bunch of steers at a water hole and rode toward them, only to see the animals break from the water in sudden alarm. The steers ran wild, their tails standing high over their backs; and, since they came straight toward the riders, Fat knew that it wasn't he and Miguel who had stampeded them.

128

The riders rode around a shoulder of rock and saw a bloody-rumped steer fleeing in panic. And just behind him, at the edge of the water, stood a big black bear with the steer's tail sticking out of his mouth.

They had no guns; the Mexican government wouldn't allow guns in that country for fear of a revolution. So all Fat and Miguel could do was hold their snorting horses while they watched the bear eat the tail, bone, hide, and all, down to the brush.

That's when Fat got his idea. Since they had nothing with which to shoot that bear, why not rope and drag the tail-eating scoundrel to death?

He offered the idea to Miguel for consideration. Miguel was game. They took down their ropes and spurred toward the bear.

Up to that time, Fat had always looked upon a bear as a big clumsy animal, without a lot of get-up-and-go to him. But the instant the bear became aware of them, he took to some shoulder-high brush and left out in a rolling gallop that ate up distance in a surprising hurry. Fat and Miguel had to spur hard to get their mounts in roping distance; and then, for some reason, they couldn't seem to get a rope on their quarry. Looked like the bear could sense the instant they hurled a loop. Every time, he'd duck to one side or the other, just enough to let the ropes settle over a bush instead of around his neck.

The bear led them in a brush-popping run up a long slant and plunged out of sight down the opposite slope. An instant later, Fat and Miguel topped out the rise, right where two draws headed up against the hill and fanned out in different directions. Since the bear wasn't in sight, the two riders parted, Fat going down the right one in a hoof-clattering ride, while Miguel went to the left.

Brush snatched and clawed at Fat, nearly dragging him out of the saddle. Then suddenly he was in the clear, and right there, in good roping distance, was the running bear. Fat let out a yell, swung his loop, and latched on.

Maybe, if Fat's horse hadn't fallen to staves, they could have jerked that bear down and dragged him to death, as Fat had planned. But like it was, the sight and smell of that big wild animal so close at hand was more than the horse could stand. He snorted and whirled aside, lost his footing and piled up with a grunt.

Fat landed on all fours, clear of the saddle, all right; but when he looked up, there came the bear, straight at him, walking on his hind legs and uttering coughing roars of rage at the rope that he was trying to claw from one shoulder.

As Fat puts it, he "raised running" and kept running, for he was dead certain that he could feel the hot breath of that angry bear on the back of his neck.

For the next hundred yards or better, Fat Alford set the speed record for short-legged cowhands outrunning bears. And it wasn't on any cinder track, either; but over ground cluttered with tall brush and boulders that would give a horse trouble to stand up on. But that didn't bother Fat, because right behind him he could hear that mad bear coming.

He rounded a shoulder of a hill and ran into Miguel, who'd heard him holler and was trying to get back into the chase. There, Fat got the courage to look behind him and discovered, to his vast relief, that it hadn't been the bear running so close behind him, after all. It had been his frightened horse.

Miguel had to run Fat's spooked horse down and rope him, and when he led him back Fat noticed that only a part of his rope was still tied to the saddle horn. He reckoned the bear was wearing the rest.

But while a rope is a mighty important part of a cowhand's equipment, Fat didn't have to study long to decide that the part the bear had was the shortest end and not really worth going back after.

They had about half the steers rounded up when Reynolds sent word to call off the gather. It seems that the price of cattle had dropped still lower, here in the States. On top of that, the U. S. government had raised the duty on imported cattle. And, what with the squeeze coming from both sides that way, Reynolds found himself in the position of having fat cattle in Mexico that wouldn't bring enough in the United States market to pay the import duty.

18

NOW that he had a car to get about in, Fat took up more or less permanent quarters at Ozona, the "Biggest Little Town in the World," according to a sign on the courthouse square.

Fat wasn't nearly so concerned about the size of the town (today its inhabitants number only about 3,500) as he was by the fact that a lot of big ranch owners, like the Hoovers, the Childresses, the Hendersons, the Phillipses, and the Baggetts were moving off their ranches into new homes they'd built in the little pecan-shaded town among the flat-topped limestone hills. These, along with the Davidsons and Wests and Kincaids and Shannons and Couches, and others who'd come early to this region, now owned most of Crockett County, not to mention various surrounding counties. Most of them had come when land could be bought for a dollar an acre or leased for a nickel an acre per year. They had lived out in brush huts and dugouts. They had tailed up poor cows and bottle-fed dogie lambs and fought off predatory cats and wolves and men and suffered drouths and loneliness and slave labor till finally livestock prices had soared.

Then, along came the discovery of oil, to increase their incomes a hundred times over what their livestock brought them; so now they were suddenly fabulously rich, with more money than they knew what to do with.

And while some blew in a lot of it on fine homes and churches and clothes and diamonds and automobiles and whiskey and women, most of them had been hard-working ranchmen too long to be anything else. So they'd used their money to buy more ranches and more cattle and sheep to stock them with.

And, of course, this required the hiring of more cowhands, which is where Fat came in.

Using his car, Fat worked over possibly a wider area of the trans-Pecos than he ever had before. But now, when a job played out, he took to coming back to Ozona to look for work. He'd learned that it was about the best place in West Texas to start looking.

Fat was in Ozona when he got word of his father's death. The old man had died in Phoenix, Arizona. He and Fat's brother, E. C., who was about nineteen, had gone to South Texas in the late summer to pick cotton and had followed the harvest that far north before the old man had contracted meningitis. It was the disease that had killed his first wife.

Fat got his friend Walter Capps to go out to Phoenix with him to help bury the old man. They arrived in the middle of the night, to learn that there'd been an epidemic in Phoenix, and that not less than sixty-five victims of meningitis lay that night awaiting burial.

Fat found his father's body in a funeral home and waited there the rest of the night till E. C. came. E. C. told him what had happened. He said that he and his father had been camping in a tent with some other cotton pickers when a boy in a neighboring tent had come down with a fever. Nobody else had paid much attention to it, but Julius Alford was pretty sure of the symptoms. He'd seen meningitis before.

The boy had no folks there, or anybody particularly interested in looking after him, so Alford had taken over. The boy didn't have money for a doctor, but Alford and E. C. couldn't help that way. They'd been sending all their money home. So Fat's father had doctored the kid the best he knew how and stayed up nights, waiting on him. But within a week the boy had died.

A few nights later, before E. C. hardly had time to realize that his father was sick, Julius Alford had died.

They buried him there at Phoenix, Fat and Walter Capps and E. C. and a cotton-picking friend of E. C.'s. There wasn't anything else they could do. The disease had reached epidemic proportions, and they couldn't get a permit to ship his body back to Coleman, Texas, where the family lived.

Fat went home to try to straighten things out for his mother and the smaller children with her. Somebody would have to provide for them. Besides E. C., who was just home now and then, Juanita was the oldest. She was fifteen, pretty, and a handful for her mother to manage. Cynthia, nine, was still little and frail and needed extra care. Little fat six-year-old Bessie was the only one who gave her mother no trouble at all and was even a little help in looking after the baby Dolorece, who toddled everywhere and got into everything.

Larence and some of the married girls might be able to help a little at times, but they had families of their own. They'd find it difficult to come up, month after month, with the cold cash necessary for the keep of

134

their mother and the four little ones. Fat decided he was the one to take over that job. He'd been sending home a little money now and then, for a good while; but mostly just when he took a notion. He hadn't ever felt responsible before. But now, somebody had to feel responsible.

It looked like when he first came home that his mother was going to get a little break in her favor. His father had kept a fifteen-hundred-dollar life insurance policy paid up. With that, Fat and his mother planned to buy her a little home somewhere, which would sure cut down on the money she'd need for house rent. But when they filed the claim on the policy, the insurance company outfigured them. The company couldn't show where the old man had ever failed to make a payment or had borrowed a cent on it, but they could point to a section of fine print in the policy that whittled the collection down to a hundred and sixty-five dollars.

Fat guessed he could take the thing to court and win the case; but he knew that by the time he'd fought it through his lawyer fees would just about take up the difference.

"Forget it, Mama," he said. "We're whipped on that one before we start. You just give me a little time; I'll get you all a place to stay."

Before he got away, some of the married girls, in an attempt to help, suggested that they split up the family. One offered to take the mother, and others offered to take one or two of the children each. But something about that riled Fat. He'd never lived at home much; yet, maybe for that very reason, home and family

135

seemed mighty important to him. He couldn't stand the thought of breaking it up.

"Hell, no!" he flared in a sudden storming rage. "Them little kids belong with Mama and that's where they're going to stay. I'll make 'em a living!"

He went back to Ozona and got himself another riding job. He swapped for a couple of ponies, took them out to the sheep ranch where he worked, broke them to ride in his spare time, then sold them for a little profit. In about six months, he was able to make a down payment on a little house and lot at Christoval, on the South Concho River. The house had only three rooms, but one of them was big and long. His mother and the children could be comfortable there.

Alice Alford was disappointed when Fat came to move her and the children. "But, son," she protested, "couldn't you have found us a place at Ozona, where we could be closer to you?"

Fat shook his head. "Mama," he said, "Ozona's a millionaire town. Everybody there owns a big ranch or oil well or both. Them people have got money to spend, and that's why I can get jobs there. But if I took you all out there and had to try to dress the girls like those kids can dress, I couldn't do it, and the girls would be miserable.

"Christoval, though, is a cheap town to live in. Nobody there has much money to spend. The girls won't feel any poorer there, especially, than anybody else."

His mother was still disappointed, yet suddenly proud of her son for his straight thinking on a matter that had never entered her mind. She wondered how her wild, harum-scarum firstborn had ever settled down enough to come by such insight. But the fact that he had gave her the confidence to do as he directed. She moved into the little house at Christoval, with the warm feeling of still having a man at the head of the family.

19

THOSE Reynolds cattle that wouldn't sell for enough money in Texas to pay their way across the Rio Grande—that was the first real indication Fat got to what was taking place in the livestock business, along with everything else.

He'd known there was a Depression making the rounds, or a Hoover Boom, as some of the politicians called it. He'd heard talk and read about it in the newspapers. But a cowhand lying up in a shack in some out-of-the-way place, trying to read a month-old paper by the light of a smoky coal-oil lamp—it's hard for him to get the real meaning out of a newspaper story. He can read about a money panic back East, but that means mighty little to him. That world's too far away, and he's never had any money to speak of, anyhow.

What if some big stock broker did jump head-first through his penthouse window and scatter his brains all over the sidewalk? To a cowhand's way of thinking, it probably served the silly fool right for not having any better sense.

But when good fat cattle won't bring enough money in Texas to pay import duty for getting them out of Mexico, that's something else. That's bringing the Depression too close to home. If a cowman can't make money out of his cattle, how is he going to pay a cowhand wages? And if a cowhand can't draw wages, how's he going to provide for a family?

Questions like that can set a man to thinking, set him to worrying, if he isn't careful. But Fat had never been the worrying kind. As the jobs began to get scarce, he began to rustle harder and hold onto his money better.

He'd never been one to blow in a lot on whiskey and women; now he cut that out altogether. He made his haircuts last twice as long. He washed his work clothes in a stock tank instead of sending them to a laundry. If he wore a hole in the seat of his pants, he patched it. If he broke a rope, he tied it back together, even though the lumpy knot threw it off balance and made roping more difficult. If he had to take a job where the ranch owner paid like he was scared to death a cowhand might get four bits ahead, he took the job and made the best of it.

For the first time in Fat's life, he wasn't just tipping his hat and riding off from jobs that didn't suit him.

As cattle prices plunged, throwing the ranch owners into a financial bind, more and more of them turned to sheep growing. Wool wasn't any big price, either, but on the forty or fifty acres it took to graze a cow that would raise only one calf, a rancher could run four or five ewes, from which he had a chance to sell that many lambs, plus a clipping of wool.

Fat held a true cowhand's dislike for the stinking, blatting, grass-killing, worm-infested, die-for-no-reason creatures. But wool growers would pay him wages to work sheep, so he worked sheep.

Most of the work consisted of rounding up and dipping and stomach worming, and always the owners

139

were in a hurry. And while they didn't exactly expect a hand to go off behind a hill and dig his grave, at the same time they sure tried to keep the coffin lid raised between him and town.

It was round up sheep by the thousands. Run a horse to death in wet times, because no sheep drives in the rain. Dry times, it was run them in the pens and eat their dust that boiled up from their hoofs and stood a quarter-mile high in the air. Crowd them through the chutes. Catch each one as he came bolting through, with his head down, aiming to butt a man flat of his back, and often doing it. Grab him by the wool and hold him. Poke a worm drench down his throat, or pitch him bodily into a dipping vat. Turn him loose and grab the next one.

And all the time, the sun is getting hotter and the sweat's dripping from a man's eyebrows and soaking his shirt, and the stench is getting stronger and the dust fog thicker and the shouts of the men and the plaintive cries of thousands of sheep are a constant din of sound, and over and through it all swarm the flies, biting and stinging.

Finally, it's night, and a man drags his bone-aching body out of the pens and heads for supper, walking bent for fifty yards before he can get the stoop out of his back.

If there's a big water tank handy, he can take a bath; if not, all he can do is wash his hands and face before he grabs a bite to eat.

Then it's hit the sack in a dirty bunkhouse and pass out faster than a drunk. Unless a man happens to land in one of the bunkhouses like the one on a ranch below

Ozona, where the bedbugs commence swarming out of the walls at nightfall, trailing a man to his bed like ants coming to fried bacon. Then all a cowhand can do is get up and burn his bedroll and lie out on the hard ground for the balance of the night, listening to the eternal blatting of the sheep and wondering how in the hell he can stretch his wages enough to pay for more bedding.

Or, if he's not suffering too bad with weariness and fly bites, he might chuckle a little over that yarn Cal Parker tells about the horse he tried to buy off the Mexican.

Cal says, "Manuel, you want to sell that horse?"

Manuel says, "Si, Señor, I sell."

"Well," Cal says, "I'll give you fifteen dollars for him."

Manuel falls back like he's been struck between the eyes with the butt end of a quirt.

"Oh, no, no, no!" Manuel says. "I no can sell for such dollars. Why, Señor Cal, I work ninety days in August for that horse!"

If a man doesn't get the point of that story, all he has to do is side Manuel in a sheep pen during the month of August. After that, he'll understand.

Sheep work has a lot in common with cotton picking.

There was this old gal we'll call Sister Grace, because that's not her name. She operated a sheep and cow outfit out of Big Lake. It wasn't as big as some ranch outfits in that country, but it was fair-sized. There were ninety-four sections of land in the horse trap.

141

Well, Sister Grace was as pious as all hell. She prayed in front of every meal. She also took a warm personal interest in the amount of food that her Negro ranch cook prepared for the cowhands in her pay. Every morning she'd be up long before daylight so that she herself could slice the ham and count the eggs and measure out the coffee.

Each cowhand got a whole slice from one of those half-sized "picnic" shoulders, cut so trim and thin that he could read a newspaper through it; each man got one whole fried egg, good or bad; and he got all the weak, sugarless, creamless coffee he could hold.

While the cowhands gorged themselves at this groaning board, Sister Grace would stand by to see that they ate it all and to give them advice on how to save money. As an example, she told them how, when she drove her Pierce-Arrow into Fort Worth, she always saved parking money. She did this by driving around till she found a free parking space somewhere, and then she'd take the two bits she'd have spent at the parking lot and transfer it from the ranch account she held jointly with her son into her personal savings account.

Such little pearls of advice were highly appreciated by the cowhands. It kept them in conversation for days. It helped them to save all the money they accumulated from their handsome wages of two dollars a day.

A saddle only cost them a hundred dollars. They could get a good pair of boots for twenty and a hat for ten and a bridle for around five and a saddle blanket for, say, ten, and a rope for two. After that, what a cowhand made was just velvet, except for having to buy a few clothes, work gloves, a bedroll, a little smoking tobacco, and maybe send a few dollars to a widowed mother and some kids. Still, if a man got careless with his wages, he might run a little low at times, so it was nice to have some thoughtful person like Sister Grace to teach them the true value of thrift.

Sister Grace kept all her cowhands well mounted, too. She'd sent a man down to Presidio, on the Rio Grande, to buy some horses at bargain prices and of a size to make it real easy for even a short-legged cowhand like Fat to mount them. The biggest horse in the bunch wouldn't have weighed more than seven hundred pounds. And since Fat, for instance, now weighed only two hundred and ten, and his saddle rigging around sixty, he usually didn't have to spur one of these horses longer than a couple of minutes before the animal could strike a gallop and hold it for at least a hundred yards. And, while these ponies were a little lightweight for heavy roping, still, if a man roped a cow weighing better than a thousand pounds and she jerked the pony off his feet, she generally didn't drag him far before he lodged against a tree or boulder and pulled her to a stop.

Altogether, Sister Grace made life so pleasant and easy for her working cowboys that some of them became almost ashamed to take pay for their work.

"I got to where," one conscience-stricken rider confided to Fat, "I just have to back up to Sister Grace on payday. Git to thinking about all them easy wages we're drawing, and I just ain't got the gall to look her in the eyes when she pays me."

But there are always some cowhands who don't know

how to appreciate a good thing. Like Fat, for instance, who lost half a night's sleep cutting out a key to fit the lock on the smokehouse door, then stealing one ham after another and carrying them off in his saddlebags and cooking them over a fire he and the other hands built out on the range somewhere. Cooking and eating that good woman's hams, when he ought to've been at work. And never even bothering to pray over it first!

What made it even worse was the way Lee Childress, who was ramrodding Sister Grace's crew of hands, would let a man like Fat get by with murder.

Take the time Fat and Kay Black ran that bunch of wormy mares in the pen to doctor them. Fat was down in the pen afoot when he roped the first one. He was using a rope with a big knot in the middle of it.

This mare made a run past him, and he reached out and picked up her forefeet; and when he did, that big knot flopped over and pulled the rope up in a tight half hitch around his left arm. Fat sensed the danger at once and tried to run with the mare till he could get free of the rope; but she took up the slack too quick and jerked him down and went to dragging him around the pen, filling his mouth with fresh cow manure as she went.

Kay Black finally got her stopped and nearly choked himself on his tobacco cud, trying to keep from laughing at Fat's predicament. Which didn't help Fat's feelings a bit. He got loose from the half hitch and gathered up his rope, which had fallen from the mare's feet when she'd stopped running, and went and climbed on his saddled horse standing close by. He made a run at the mare and she lit out in a high-tailed gallop around the pen again, and Fat reached out and laid the loop on.

144

But this time he had a tight wrap around his saddle horn; when the mare ran out to the end of the rope, Fat couldn't have lifted her up by the tail and stood her on her head any neater.

She took a buster against the ground, just like Fat aimed for her to, and Fat turned and rode off across the pen, dragging her up close, so Kay wouldn't have so far to walk with the worm medicine. Kay brought the medicine and went to dabbing it in the wormy wound, and by that time Fat had dragged his shirt sleeve against his mouth and wiped out enough cow manure that he could talk again.

"Kay," he said. "I think you're wasting that worm medicine."

Kay stood up and took a closer look at the mare, then kicked her in the belly. When she didn't move a muscle, he turned to Fat and nodded.

"Think you're right, Fat," he said. "Looks like she's done cured for good."

About that time Sister Grace, with Lee Childress riding beside her, herded her Pierce-Arrow up to the pen and demanded to know what on earth had happened to the mare.

Kay Black shook his head in worried concern and told Sister Grace that the only thing he could figure could have killed the mare was the worm medicine. "That stuff is just too strong, I do believe," he said gravely.

Lee Childress, who could read the signs there in Fat's smeared face and all over the scuffed-up dirt in the pen, could have got Fat fired by pointing out that the mare's neck was broken. Instead, he handed Fat one of his

145

famous lopsided grins and said he'd had his suspicions all along about that off-brand worm medicine that Sister Grace had been buying at bargain prices.

Finally Sister Grace let her lease run out, and some finance company took it up to get a place to run all the thousands of sheep they'd had to repossess on some bad loans they'd made to wool growers.

Sister Grace waited till she had only a few weeks to get off the ranch, then called on the hands to make a two-month roundup in about three weeks. She even had to hire on some extra help, which was torture to her saving nature.

Any given number of cowhands, even working double time and running a lot of good stock to death in their hurry, can handle just so many cows and horses and sheep in any given number of days. When at the end of a month's time the cowhands still weren't done, Sister Grace fired the whole crew.

However, her son managed to hire them all back with the promise that he'd take the chuckwagon out where they wouldn't have to put up with the old woman till they'd finished the gather.

They were still a week from being done, and out of grub, too, on the day that Tom Owens, who was to manage the ranch for the finance company, came to take possession. So they drove in for any provisions that might be left in the smokehouse and got there in time for Sister Grace's departure.

When they arrived, they found Owens and his wife and two little girls camped in a swarm of flies out under a hackberry tree about a hundred yards from the house.

Around them, sitting out in the hot sun, was all their furniture. And walking around all this was Tom Owens, grinding his teeth and swearing under his breath because he'd made the mistake of bringing his family out here three days before he could legally take possession of the house.

The old ranch house was big enough to accommodate three families; Sister Grace had already stripped it of her own furniture and had her suitcases packed and loaded into the Pierce-Arrow. But she wasn't letting anybody move into that house a minute before she got ready to leave.

The cowhands found her gathering up the last bits and scraps of food in the kitchen and smokehouse. Her son asked her what she was going to do with that food, and she told him she was taking it to town to sell it back to the groceryman she'd bought it from.

Her son said, "But, Mama, we'll need that grub in camp." He began loading some cans of hominy and corn and tomatoes into a big box.

Sister Grace looked at him like he was stealing something, but she said nothing until he lifted out a good-sized sack of potatoes. "Not those!" she said then, and grabbed the sack. "You know you can't fool with peeling and cooking potatoes in camp." She started to the car with the potatoes.

At that, the son lifted a whole case of tomatoes from a shelf and handed them to Fat. "Take that to the chuckwagon," he ordered, then stepped out of the house for a moment.

Fat had barely got out the door with the tomatoes before Sister Grace was back. "Put them over there," she ordered, indicating the pile of groceries she was loading into the car.

Then she left out with another load of stuff and her son came back in. "I thought I told you to take those tomatoes out to the chuckwagon," he said to Fat.

Fat said that was right, he just hadn't got around to it yet. He picked up the tomatoes and started out with them again, following the son, who was carrying other groceries out. But he hadn't got far with them when back came Sister Grace.

"Didn't I tell you to put those tomatoes over in that pile?" she demanded.

Fat said, "Yessum," and put the tomatoes back.

That went on and on until Fat finally got a chance to slip out to the salthouse, where he hid the crate of tomatoes. This seemed like such a good idea that he went back for another load of groceries and slipped them into the salthouse, too, and then another one.

Sister Grace began to suspect something. She went over to the chuckwagon and demanded to see every parcel of food in the chuckbox. Of course, with Fat's taking it all out to the salthouse, the chuckbox didn't look too overloaded. She went back and searched the kitchen and smokehouse, but didn't find anything.

Finally, she climbed into the Pierce-Arrow and took a last look around. And that's when she was suddenly overcome with the sadness of leaving. She broke into tears and was uttering great sobs of grief as she drove away.

Fat and Kay Black were almost overcome with grief, too, at seeing her go.

"Wouldn't it be a shame," Fat remarked, "if the poor

old soul was to happen to hit that bump-gate too hard and it would swing around and smear her all over that road?"

The horror of such a possibility made Kay cry out in protest. "No, man! Think of all the poor cowhands in hell. They've got enough to put up with, like it is."

But Sister Grace made it safely through the tricky bump-gate and went on her way. And Fat and Kay made a run for the salthouse, where they went to hauling out groceries and drooling over the glorious prospects of getting a full meal for a change.

20

FOR weeks, Fat had been laying off to pay a visit to Christoval to see how his mother and the kids were making out. But seemed like he couldn't get time. He was trying to send his mother forty dollars a month for running expenses and still keep up payments on that house he'd bought them. And, with jobs scarce and pay getting scarcer, it seemed like he was kept in a long lope all the time.

Then one day he was out at the Alpine stockyards, helping a man named Ferguson shape up a bunch of fat calves for shipping. There were about five hundred head of these calves, and Fat was trying to get them classed and separated for size and flesh. He was working out in the middle of a long alley between two pens when a train pulled in. The train was snorting and puffing. The wheels were clattering on the rails. And, as if this weren't enough, the fool engineer had to take a notion to pull the whistle cord just then.

That sudden piercing blast of sound was too much for the calves. They spooked. A bunch of them came stampeding out of one pen, heading for the next. Fat was trapped in the alley where he couldn't get out. And the weight of all those wild-scared calves, ramming into his horse, was more than the animal could stand against. Down he went, carrying Fat with him. And

150

over the two of them went the herd—all five hundred head, it seemed to Fat.

Trampling hoofs cut and tore at his face, belly, chest, and arms. They crushed him with their weight. They smothered him with their body heat and with the choking fog of manure dust they churned up from the ground.

Then, just as it looked like he couldn't last for another instant, there was a splitting and crashing sound, and the whole side of a pen went down under the press of weight. The calves poured through, and Fat was in the clear.

He was a sorry sight, but he was in luck. He was cut and bruised from head to foot. His nose was broken, and blood leaked through his shirt and pants. But he wasn't dead!

However, it was going to be a while before he could straddle a horse again. Even he could see that. He guessed there wasn't anything now to keep him from making that trip home to Christoval.

So he piled his battered body into his Model T and headed for Christoval. And while he was bothered some about the wages he wasn't making, he sure found it nice to lie around the house and have his mama fussing over his cuts and hurts, and to eat woman-cooked grub again and pick on the little kids, Cynthy and Bessie and Dolorece.

Cynthia was ten, mighty little and puny-looking, while Bessie was only seven, but big and stout for her age. The two of them were about like Fat and his next younger brother, Benny, had been when they were kids, back there on the Colorado River.

151

Fat lay in bed and chuckled, thinking how it had been with him and Benny in those days. Benny had been big for his age—as big at eight as Fat was at twelve. So Fat, being older, had had to keep proving that he could whip Benny. And Benny, who was always scary, hadn't liked to fight; but once Fat got him cornered, Benny could sure give a good account of himself. . . .

Fat had been pestering Benny for a week. Scaring him mostly. Pushing him off into deep water where Benny was afraid to go. Jeering at him because he wouldn't climb a tall tree. Poking a stick at him through the weeds, hollering "Snake!" and then dying with laughter when Benny took to his heels in terror. Crowding him till he'd finally turn and fight. Trying hard to give him a good sound thrashing, but never quite getting the job done.

After so long, their father stepped in. "All right, you boys," he said. "I'm tired of this constant wrangling and fighting. I want you to kiss and make up."

Fat was horrified. "Do what?"

"I want you to kiss each other," their father said.

Fat was stunned. He couldn't imagine anything more humiliating than kissing his brother Benny. With the rest of the family all looking on and grinning.

He looked at Benny. It was plain from the expression on Benny's face that he wasn't in a kissing mood. But it was equally plain that Benny was scared not to.

"Go on. Get at it," their father ordered.

Benny puckered up and came at Fat with hate in

152

his eyes. He gave Fat a quick peck on the cheek, then jerked away as if he'd just kissed a toad.

All the rest of the kids snickered and giggled.

"All right, Eddie," Alford said to Fat. "It's your turn now. Go ahead and kiss your brother."

Fat went ahead. He grabbed Benny and held him and bit his cheek like a dog catching a varmint.

Benny fell back howling. Fat hit for the door, but didn't quite make it. One of his father's hands shut down on his arm like a vise and the other one reached up to unhook a razor strop from a nail on the wall.

When he got through and called on Fat again to kiss his brother, Benny's fat cheek had sure looked a lot more kissable.

Bessie, though—she wasn't scary like Benny had been. Bessie would try anything. And Cynthy, who didn't like to have a younger sister able to do everything she did, was generally daring Bessie to do something just to show her that she couldn't.

They were playing out there in the yard—Cynthy and Bessie, around an old fire-blackened washpot.

Cynthy dared, "Bet you can't jump over that old washpot. Bet you're too big and fat."

Bessie got red in the face. "Bet I'm not too fat!" she declared; then she ran and jumped, barely clearing the washpot. "Now let's see you jump it!"

Cynthy ran and jumped, so sure she could clear the washpot that she didn't try hard. So she landed right in the middle of it and cut her lip and skinned her nose and started screaming bloody murder.

Fat crippled outside to drag Cynthy out of the pot

153

and try to hush her up by wooling her around and making like her hurts didn't amount to anything. Which only made her cry louder, so that his mother had to come and take over. And while she was getting Cynthy quieted down, Fat started a romp in the middle of the floor with Bessie. He got down on his hands and knees and had her climb astride his back.

"Now," he said, "I'm a bronc and you're a broncbuster; so you hang and rattle."

He cut loose, pitching and bawling, never for a minute thinking Bessie couldn't ride him, and threw her nearly to the ceiling. She landed on the floor, more scared than hurt; but that didn't matter. Now, he had Bessie screaming bloody murder, too.

Then one night, Juanita, who was about sixteen, slipped off and went to a dance down at the depot, where she'd been playing a French harp, along with a kid fiddler named Grady Steiger and her brother E. C., who picked a guitar. She stayed out all night. When she came home in the morning, Fat didn't listen to her explanation of how the big rain that had fallen during the night put the Concho up and cut her off from home, so that she'd had to stay all night with a girl friend. Fat was too angry. He tore into her with a razor strop to teach her a lesson. She was his kid sister, and no kid sister of his was going to a dance and stay out all night.

Used to dealing with horses and cattle, Fat wasn't thinking how heavy-handed he was with that strop till his mother stepped in and took the strop from his hands.

After that, the girls got to stepping pretty light and easy around their older brother.

154

Fat wasn't quite aware of it at first, not till one day when E. C. came home.

E. C. had been off on a job somewhere and made a little money and used part of it to buy himself a bottle of bootleg booze. He came in, about three sheets in the wind, which always made him so big-hearted and full of fun that Fat could hardly raise a fuss with him about throwing his money away on hooch, even with money as scarce as it was. E. C. had candy in his pockets for the little girls and a fistful of chicken-feed change for them, too, and some sort of doodad present for Juanita and a lot of good-natured hoorawing for his mother.

The whole bunch swarmed over him like he was the long-lost son, even though he'd been gone less than a week. And watching that gave Fat a sort of lonely, left-out feeling, making him more than ever aware of how his younger sisters were avoiding him.

The feeling hung on; it was still with him when he finally got well and was fixing to go back to work again.

He asked his mother, "Mama, how come the kids don't seem to have much liking for me?"

Alice Alford knew instinctively what Fat was thinking. Here he was, the breadwinner of the family, yet not loved like some of the others.

"Son," she said, "you're too rough with them. They don't get to see you often and then, when they do, you're so rough you scare them to death."

Fat did some sober thinking on that one as he headed West again. He guessed his mama was right, he was too rough. He'd been born rough, and the kind of work he did made him rougher. And, as a rider by the name of Phil Maddux had once commented to him, "A

155

West Texas cowhand has to be as rough and tough as a boot heel to stay in the roundup."

But when it came to dealing with kids, Fat wished he could learn to gentle down a little. It'd be sort of nice to come in home and have the family swarm all over him, like they'd done E. C.

21

ON his return to Ozona, Fat got a job pumping water for a bunch of steers that Charlie Davidson and his father, Judge Davidson, had on the graze, south of town.

Up until the Depression, a lot of cowhands were too bowlegged for this kind of work. Any job they couldn't handle from the back of a horse was hardly good enough for them. But hard times began to straighten out a lot of those saddle-bent legs, so that windmill repairing or fence building came more natural to cowhands than it once had.

Fat's legs had never been too badly warped in this respect; and right now, after losing so many weeks' work, he didn't feel that he could afford to be choosey. He'd draw wages and eat; and, from what he'd heard and read, there were a whole lot of people in the United States right then who weren't doing either very often.

He had three separate big tanks to keep full by pumping water into them from nearby wells. The well pumps were powered by gasoline engines; and if Man ever invented a machine more tricky and cantankerous and unreasonable than water-pump engines, Fat had never had any dealings with it up to this time. Still, with a lot of backbreaking cranking and colorful profanity and frequent applications of grease and oil to both the

157

engines and himself, Fat got along well enough to draw his wages.

Where the job fell short of his expectations was in the matter of grub.

Charlie Davidson had told Fat he could board with the folks living there on the ranch; and Fat found that when those folks were at home, they fed well enough. Where the rub came in was the fact that they so seldom stayed home. And every time they left, seemed like it was on the day that the groceries had all played out. Sometimes it looked to Fat like maybe they'd just loaded up what groceries there were in the kitchen and hauled them off with them.

Fat could hardly afford to leave his engines long enough to go in and complain to Charlie. So when the folks were gone, he'd knock over a rabbit or a squirrel when he could, and go hungry the rest of the time.

Once, after these folks had been gone from home better than a week, Charlie Davidson happened to show up out there. This was lucky for Fat, on account of a valve had just gone out in one of the pump cylinders, which called for a lot of rod pulling and was a bigger job than one man could well handle by himself. So Charlie pitched in and helped Fat, and by working right on through dinnertime to around two o'clock in the afternoon, they finally completed the repairs and had water pouring into the tank for the thirst-bawling steers beginning to crowd around.

Charlie backed off from the job, as worn-out and greasy and rust-spattered as Fat, and allowed they might ought to drive to the house now and get a bite to eat. And that's when Fat recollected that all the grub he had at the house was the short end of a sack of flour and some bacon grease. But, being a gentleman, Fat wasn't the sort to apologize to a guest for the meager fare he had to set out. He just rode with Charlie to the house, where he washed up and started mixing a batch of biscuits.

Charlie got the fire going in the cookstove and asked Fat where the coffee was, and Fat said he was just fresh out. Then Charlie started looking for the bacon, and Fat had to explain that he was fresh out of that, too. Finally, Charlie asked Fat what they were going to eat, and Fat studied for a little bit and came up with an idea.

"I tell you what, Charlie. There's three or four old hens hanging around the barn out there, and if they've laid today and we can find their eggs, let's have some eggs."

Charlie looked at Fat; but Charlie was a gentleman, too, and he didn't say anything. Fat shoved his biscuits into the hot oven, then they went out to the barn and searched around and were lucky. They found two eggs, and when they'd packed them back to the house and broken them, both eggs turned out to be good. So they ate biscuits and one egg apiece for dinner and topped it off with a good drink of well water and wiped their mouths on their shirt sleeves. And Charlie got up from the table and thanked Fat for the meal and Fat told him good-by and Charlie headed for town in his pickup and Fat got him some gasoline and packed it out to one of the engines and started pumping water again.

Along about sundown, Charlie was back out at the

ranch, with the rear end of his pickup full of groceries. He started unloading them and Fat helped him. When they were finally done, Charlie said solemnly, "Went in and had a little talk with my dad, and we decided that if you were going to stay out here and keep these engines going, maybe you ought to have a little something to eat every now and then."

And from then till the folks Fat was boarding with had time to come home and leave again, Fat ate pretty well.

From pumping water for Charlie Davidson, Fat went to work for Joe Davidson, where he ran into another streak of hard luck and wound up as a cook, about the lowest form of life around a cow outfit.

The trouble started because of a rodeo. Fat wanted to enter the wild-cow milking contest; so he was working double time at his regular ranch jobs to make sure everything was taken care of before he took off for the rodeo the next day. He got to crowding his horse a little too fast, and the horse stumped his toe on a boulder and turned a wildcat. The spill threw Fat against a rock and broke his collarbone.

By the time he'd mounted and dismounted to open the three gates between him and the ranch headquarters, he was feeling pretty rocky; and he was feeling a whole lot worse by the time some of the cowhands had hauled him into town to a doctor.

This doctor was an old-like fellow, not strong enough to handle the job alone. He called on Pascal Northcutt, a druggist, and another man by the name of Ray Piner, to help him set the bone.

He told Fat to lie down on that table there and relax, and Fat said sure and lay down and did all the relaxing he could, under the circumstances.

Well, they went to pulling and hauling on his arm, trying to get the broken bones to fit again; but there weren't enough men to do it. They called in another man and tried again. And Fat was relaxing so hard with all that pain that he suddenly humped up and threw the whole bunch out into the middle of the floor.

This made the doctor mad. He got to his feet and said, "I thought I told you to relax."

Fat said, "Well, didn't I?"

The doctor swore a little and they tried it again, and this time Fat landed in the middle of the floor with the others.

And that did it. The jar slipped the bones back into place, as pretty as you please, so that all they had to do now was put the brace on him.

This brace consisted of a bunch of choke ropes and girths and buckles and steel supports, and by the time they'd got it cinched on him, Fat knew exactly why a young bronc fought so savagely the first time somebody tried to saddle him.

In fact, if he'd known ahead of time how it was going to be later on, he might have fought harder. He left the doctor's office and went to the house of a man he knew. The man put him to bed, and Fat went off to sleep pretty soon.

When he woke up, it was dark, and he thought he'd get up and see what time it was; but right away he found what a mistake he'd made when he'd lain down in the harness and lifted both feet off the floor. He

161

couldn't move. He was like a terrapin that'd been kicked over onto its back; he couldn't reach anything with hands or feet.

He called for help, but the man who had put him to bed had left the house; so there he lay, squirming and yelling and hollering. Finally, a boy passing along the street came in to see what all the commotion was about. He stayed to put one of Fat's feet on the floor so he could sit up.

After that scare, Fat caught on. A man doesn't want to go to bed in a harness like that unless he sleeps with one foot on the floor.

So, while some other cowhand won the purse for the wild-cow milking and drew the easy money for picking up the broncs in the bucking arena, Fat lay around in his harness, hurting. He hurt so badly that he couldn't even enjoy a visit from his family, who'd come out in a borrowed car driven by E. C., to take in the rodeo and watch Fat perform.

The only cheering thing about the whole miserable and disappointing situation was the fight that E. C. got into.

The difficulty came up when E. C. overheard a remark by some man who evidently wasn't the best friend Fat had. Talk of Fat's accident was making the rounds when this bird allowed that if Fat wasn't always acting such a reckless damned fool, he wouldn't have got hurt.

The sneering tone of this remark put E. C. on the warpath. He said nobody could talk about his brother like that with him laying up in bed, helpless; and he bowed up and proceeded to fist-whip this old boy all over a city block.

Fat was a little surprised when he heard about it. He and E. C. never had been as close as some brothers get; and it gave him a mighty warm feeling to learn that his brother held a higher opinion of him than he'd figured.

But not even this heart-warming incident took the sting out of Joe Davidson's offer to take Fat on as a ranch cook. Davidson told Fat that the ranch cook had quit on him, and he thought Fat might want the job till he was able to ride again.

To a real cowhand, the offer of a ranch cooking job is pretty much of a shock and insult. Around cow outfits, cooking is considered even lower than hole digging or windmilling. To offer a cowhand such a job is like chopping his finger off without offering him a shot of something first.

But Fat knew Davidson wasn't meaning it that way, that he was trying to help him out in a bad time; so he told the rancher he'd take the job. On the way out to the ranch, however, he made up his mind that if a one of the hands working for Davidson ever tried to hooraw him about sinking so low that he had to turn cook, he was going to strychnine the whole bunch.

They were just the kind to do it, too. There was Ted Powers and Plez Dryden and Mark Black and Bill Townsend and Bill Grimmer and Joe Tom Davidson. Not a one of them was above trying to get back at Fat for the pranks he'd pulled on them at one time or another.

But maybe they knew how he felt. Or maybe it was

the quality of the food Fat cooked. Anyhow, they all let him alone about his mishap and ate till Fat decided they didn't have but one gut and it went straight through.

Fat had two bread pans that held a hundred and five biscuits to the making, and his biscuits weren't the little old jelly-bean kind, either, like a lot of women cooks turn out. They were every one man-size. And there was plenty of beef and red beans and flour gravy and milk and ham and butter, and Fat's special: an egg custard that he always built to four-gallon size at each cooking.

But with all that grub before them, those boys kept the table stripped so bare that Joe Davidson's old shepherd dog came close to starving to death in the month's time it took Fat to get well and get back into the saddle again.

Some of those eaters talked a little about taking Fat out and breaking his collarbone again, to keep him back of the kitchen stove; but they never did get around to trying it.

22

MOST of the time, any special abilities a working
cowhand had as a roper or rider went unnoticed
by everyone except the boss he worked for and the men
he worked with. But, once a year, he participated in an
event that gave him a chance to show the world what
he could do.

This was generally on the Fourth of July, when every
ranch cook, horse wrangler, banker, school kid, drugstore soda jerker, truck driver, Mexican sheepherder,
and the cowman's diamond-studded wife turned out for
the annual rodeo and race meet.

Before this chattering, pop-drinking, barbecue-eating,
love-making, dancing, fighting, and whiskey-guzzling
crowd, gathered at the local arena, the working cowhand took his place in the sun. If he thought he was a
bronc-stomper, he got his chance at the worst broncs in
the country. If he was handy with his loop, he could
show the shouting, cheering crowd just how fast he
could rope, throw, and tie down a running calf or steer.
If he owned a fast horse, here was his chance for an
hour of glory and a fat purse if he'd laid his bets right.

Especially was this true along in the twenties and
thirties, before the rodeo got to be Big Business and
was pretty well taken over by the professionals in the
game. In those days, it was just a big casual get-
together, with little organization and with anybody

165

welcome to enter the contests, which more or less developed as the show moved along.

During those years, the town of Ozona held the reputation of holding the biggest and best rodeos in West Texas and probably deserved it. People from a radius of two hundred and fifty miles attended, year after year. They came by the thousands and came with coming appetites for the free barbecue donated by the local ranch owners. Fat remembers that, in the year of 1927, he helped to butcher two hundred and fifty goats and some fifteen fat steers for the three-day feed.

Bob Cook was in charge of the barbecuing, which was done in open pits, dug into the ground to hold the fire, and with net wire stretched across the top to support the huge chunks of meat. Cook, who's retired now, turned out such succulent meat for those affairs that his reputation spread clear back East. There, some of the big meat-packing companies heard about him and sent agents down with orders to buy his special barbecue sauce recipe. Their agents returned with the astonishing news that Cook made his meat taste that way by the simple application of salt and pepper. Cook's secret was in the long, slow cooking and in the type of wood he used.

Like the rest of the working cowhands in the country, Fat took in most of these rodeos. Usually, he participated in some of the contests. He could rope with the best, but he generally lost time in dismounting and tying his calf, so that he won only an occasional prize in this event. The contests he enjoyed most were the wildest and most reckless on the program: the wild-cow milking and the wild-mare racing.

166

He and Tom Powers' brother Ted generally teamed for the wild-cow milking. For this event, a wild cow was turned out of a chute, and two cowhands spurred hard after her; one cowhand did the roping and holding while the other did his milking into a coke bottle. Fat was the milker of his team. After being kicked half across the arena several times, he'd done some studying and figured out a way to get milk and still dodge those flailing hoofs. He'd noticed that it's virtually impossible for a cow to kick straight back, so he took to running in after she was roped and milking her from between the hind legs.

This approach gained Fat time where seconds count and saved him from a lot of bone-smashing blows. But while he often arrived at the judges' stand the winner, he seldom arrived there without a shirt collar full of fresh cow manure.

Once he and Louis Babb came close to winning a wild-mare race. Fat roped their mare out of the snorting, scrambling pen full of them and had her out on the track before even Tom Taylor and his partner, who always won this contest. And the mare wasn't cutting up any, to speak of.

They slapped a saddle on her and Fat said, "Now, Louis, climb on and coast her around before she has time to get scared. We've got this race sewed up."

Louis went up into the saddle. The mare stepped out under him pretty good. But now, here came half a dozen more men with biting, squealing, plunging mares that were fighting their ropes and running backwards over each other and the men trying to handle them, and lashing out with hard hoofs in all directions. In a minute, other men would be mounted, and here was Louis' mare, just sort of trotting along beside Fat, who was slapping her on the rump once in a while to keep her going, but still not really hurrying her.

Louis couldn't take it. He had to get more speed out of that mare. So he socked his Kelly Rogers to her; and he hadn't ought to've done it. She broke wind with a loud report and exploded like a stick of dynamite.

Fat looked up in time to see Louis spread out in the air like a great frog, and had to run to keep Louis from falling on him.

So Tom Taylor and his partner eased their mare around the track and won the race, the same as usual; and, drawing a different mare every time, won the two succeeding races.

Everybody except Fat wondered how in the devil he did it. But Fat had caught on. Tom was winning those races by doing what Fat had instructed Louis Babb to do—by easing his ponies into a run instead of spurring them into a pitching spree. Babb had just been too eager.

Fat never did consider himself a bronc-stomper, like some, and made it a practice to stay as far away as he could get from the horses brought in for the bronc-busting contests. These were bad horses, the worst outlaws produced in a country that was full of outlaw horses. If they hadn't been man-killers, they'd never have been brought in for the show.

However, Fat made one glory-getting ride before the rodeo crowd on a big gray horse named Funeral Wagon.

He hadn't planned to enter the bronc-busting. But he and a partner of his arrived at the show with their skins

168

full of brave-making Prohibition whiskey and a flat pint tucked into their boot tops for reinforcement; and the longer they watched the show, the tamer those horses appeared. The next thing Fat knew, there he was, climbing over the side of the bucking chute and easing himself down into the saddle.

The announcer hollered, "Fat Alford, coming out on Funeral Wagon!"

About that time, Fat's senses cleared a little and he thought, "Damn, I got no business here." But by then it was too late. The chute gate was flung open and out they came, with Funeral Wagon bawling like a man-eating lion and trying to make a corkscrew out of his backbone with the first long leap.

That first big jump was about all Fat ever remembered. It shook up that belly-load of whiskey till Fat's brain just seemed to soar out of his head. He didn't hear the time whistle blow and just vaguely remembers being dragged out of the saddle and of sliding to the ground off the rump of the pickup man's horse.

After that, everything went blank again, till he came to over at the side of the arena. Somebody was shaking him by the shoulder and saying, "Man, you won some money that ride!"

Fat said, "The hell I did!"

The man told him he'd better get on up to the judges' stand; so Fat went reeling off in that direction. He was stopped just under the stand by a revenue officer, who said, "What's that running out of your boot, man?"

Fat glanced down. "Why," he said in surprise, "it looks like blood, don't it?"

"Yeah, but it smells like whiskey," the officer said. "Pull that boot off."

That's when Fat recollected the pint of whiskey he'd been carrying in his boot top.

Under the accusing gaze of the Prohibition officer, he reached down and slipped off his boot. Out of it poured a mixture of blood and whiskey, followed by a tinkling of chips of glass.

"Why that damned old horse!" Fat exclaimed. "Slammed me agin something and busted my water bottle!"

With the ground soaking up the evidence, there wasn't any way the officer could prove in court that Fat had been carrying whiskey. So Fat went on up and collected his money for making a prize-winning ride on Funeral Wagon, and the purse was of a size to keep him in whiskey for the duration of the rodeo.

The Ozona rodeos generally lasted for three days, during which most everybody got his fill of eating and drinking and fist-fighting and making love down in the big draw south of town. So they all went home, where they could rest up and start making plans for the big blowout they'd pull off next year.

23

THE Depression grew worse. Big ranches folded and went under. Jobs became more and more scarce. Fat scrambled harder. He helped his brother E. C. to locate jobs. Any kind of a job, from stump grubbing to fence building. And still it wasn't enough. They lost that house and lot Fat bought for his mother at Christoval. Together, Fat and E. C. couldn't get enough work to keep up the payments.

Fat moved the family into a rent house, then headed West in his Model T, on the lookout for whatever sort of work he might run across.

At Fort Davis he found a job. A rancher by the name of George Young said he had work for several men. He said he and a man named Estes had a bunch of cattle on a lease in the Apache Indian Reservation of Arizona. They were fixing to round the cattle up and sell them and they needed riders to make the gather. The only thing was, Young said, he and Estes had no money to pay their riders. And, the way things looked then, they might not have any after they'd sold the cattle. But they could feed a crew, and if the hands wanted to take a chance on the cattle's selling for enough profit to pay wages, then he and Estes could sure use them.

Along with some other riders, Fat took the chance. There wasn't much else he could do. He didn't know of another job in the country; and if he had, he was too broke to buy gasoline to get to it. So he went with Young to Arizona to gather Double Circle cattle out of the Mogollon Mountains.

Young and Estes had a big stretch of country under lease there; it reached about seventy-five miles in one direction and sixty-five in another. It was too big to work with one crew, of course; so the Double Circle bosses divided their forty riders into four separate crews and sent them into various parts of the mountains.

The crews couldn't get wagons into such high, rough country; so they loaded their camping plunder onto pack mules, which they drove ahead of them, along with the *remuda* of big mountain horses.

Fat's crew pitched camp high up among the big pines, where the nights were frosty cold and the mountain slopes were so steep-slanted that Fat couldn't see how a horse stood up on one, much less caught a cow on it. But once they'd started work, he got a surprise. And that's when he came to appreciate the big raw-boned iron-jawed horses he'd been so doubtful of at the start.

He got the scare of his life that first morning. Not knowing what this mountain work would be like, and being about half scared of it, Fat tried to stick fairly close to the Arizona riders in his crew, hoping to learn a little from them before going ahead on his own.

But the horse he rode had different ideas. The horse knew his work and expected the same of his rider. The first time Fat got off to himself a little and happened to jump a cow, he didn't get a chance to let somebody else take over and show him what to do. The horse just backed his ears and took after her. And the next thing

172

Fat knew, they'd plunged off the rim of a mountain, and down under them was a pine-studded grade dropping away for better than a mile at a pitch that put Fat's heart into his mouth.

But there was no stopping the horse. Fat could have hauled back on the reins till the bits split the horse's mouth clear back to his brains, and it still wouldn't have checked him. Once they'd gone off that rim, the pull of gravity had taken over.

How the horse kept his feet under him was more than Fat could understand. He'd thought he'd done some wild riding in West Texas, but this beat anything he could imagine. One second the horse's feet were on the ground, the next he'd quit the earth and risen like a deer to clear a fallen pine log that lay breast-high to him. He landed in a squat, rump to the earth, while he slid for fifty yards or better, dislodging flat rocks big as table tops that came tumbling after them. Then, as the trailing rocks gathered speed and started pitching end over end, catching up with them, the horse buck-jumped to one side to get out of their path, then went racing on down the mountain beside them.

They were halfway to the bottom when Fat finally woke up enough to realize that for the last hundred yards the horse he rode had been running with his chin over the cow's hip, waiting for him to do something about it. Fat took his cue from the horse. He quit chewing on his heart and reached out with his loop and tied on. And, about that time, they hit a piece of gentler slope, so the horse squatted and they got stopped.

After that ride, Fat felt that he'd been initiated, and never again was there any question in his mind about

173

those mountain-raised horses. They might be big and rawboned and ugly, but they knew how to keep their feet under them.

Roping a cow there in the mountains, Fat soon learned, didn't necessarily mean that a man had her caught. He could rope her and tie her to a tree and leave her there till he could gather more and bring them by. But, half the time, when he turned a wild one loose, all she did was take out in another wild run, which generally spooked the others into following her, so that he had the whole bunch to catch and rope a second or third time before he finally got them into a pen.

Now and then the riders could catch a few cattle easily by making trap pens, baited with salt, or built around some water hole. The pens were constructed out of pine or aspen logs, with the entrances so arranged that a cow could crowd through a narrow opening by pushing apart springy logs that would close in behind her. Sometimes they could even drive a cow out of the mountains if she wasn't too high up, or if they didn't happen to get attacked by some outlaw bull that had been choused around till he'd gotten ringy and would come out to fight any rider that he could smell. Then, of course, all a rider could do was let his cow go while he spurred away, trying to outrun the bull.

But mostly it was catch and rope each cow that they came across and then try to get her out of the mountains the best way they could.

Working that way, it took them a long time to round up the Double Circle cattle, because often, after working all day, twenty riders wouldn't have more than fifteen or twenty head in the pen when night fell.

How many cattle Young and Estes had in the mountains, they didn't know; and how many they finally caught, Fat never did learn. But after several months of some of the roughest and wildest riding Fat ever got into, they'd gathered and sold enough cattle to pay off the hands. Which, to Fat, right then, was the most important thing about his cow work in Arizona.

24

FAT'S mother had grown up in a time when nice girls kept their clothes on and wouldn't be seen exposing themselves to public gaze in any garb as daring and brazen as a bathing suit. And, since she'd held to that way of thinking, she'd never let Fat's older sisters learn to swim. But when Fat moved her and the younger ones to Christoval, where the south Concho River formed some of the clearest and prettiest pools ever shaded by monster live oaks, elms, and pecans, he had a talk with her. He told her there wasn't any sense in letting kids grow up without learning to swim and enjoy themselves in a river like this one, just because of some old-fashioned ideas.

His mama argued with him, but Fat argued back and finally persuaded her to let him take the younger girls down and fit them out in bathing suits.

Well, that was just fine with the girls. They took to the water like young ducks. In no time they were all swimming. Then, of course, the next time Fat pulled in home, they couldn't rest till he'd put on a borrowed bathing suit and come on down to the pool with them where they could show off how well they'd learned to swim.

They took him into the water and showed off their swimming for a while. Then they dived off the spring-

176

board and dared him to do it; so he dived off. Then he decided he'd show off to them a little.

There was a big pecan tree on the bank with high, wide-spreading branches hanging out over the water. Fat said he guessed he'd just climb that tree and show the girls what real high-diving was like.

Cynthia said if he dived from up there, she could too. Beulah, a married sister, who had come along to watch, tried to get Cynthia not to and then tried to get Fat not to let her. But Fat just laughed and told Cynthy to come on, then sort of wished he hadn't, after they'd climbed the tree and got out on that limb. It seemed like from up there, looking down, it was a whole lot further to the water than it'd seemed from down there, looking up. And the thought came to him that if he was about half afraid, then the dive must look awful scary to Cynthy.

But Cynthia and Bessie had seen him hesitate, and now they were laughing at him, calling him a "fraidy cat"; so he knew he had to make good his brag. He figured the best way to keep Cynthy from getting afraid was to act like it wasn't anything at all to dive into the water from twenty feet up.

So he climbed out a little further on a limb that sagged under his weight, and stood up to make a grand bow to his jeering audience. And, about that time, one foot slipped, and out of that tree he tumbled, striking the water boar-coon fashion: flat of his belly and all spread out.

It felt like an hour before he got his head out of the water, and another one before he got his breath back after the belly-buster. He had nearly knocked the pool dry, and, of course, his belly skin was red from slapping the water so hard. The girls shrieked their delight, and Beulah ran off laughing, and then Cynthia made her dive and it was just as pretty and smooth as a bird flying.

After that, the girls called him their Major Hoople and hounded him to death about his fancy diving, which made Fat feel good. He figured they had to think a lot of him, to wart the hell out of him the way they were doing.

25

FAT was worse broke than the Ten Commandments. He hadn't sent a dollar home to his mother in weeks. Which, of course, was exactly the right time for some of his teeth to start acting up. One tooth hurt alone for a while, then the next one to it got sympathetic and started helping it hurt. Fat needed to go to a dentist, but he'd just landed a job, for a change, with the West-Pyle Cattle Company operating out of Sanderson, and he hated taking time off when jobs were so scarce. Especially to go blow wages he hadn't drawn yet on a tooth pulling.

So he kept on working, trying to fight the pain with a regular round of swearing about twice a day, which is good enough medicine for some hurts, but doesn't seem to bring much ease to a toothache.

It was early spring, with the weather cold and raw, and the size of the ache those two teeth put out when a chill wind struck them made Fat wonder sometimes if they weren't teeth built for a horse. He hadn't had a good night's sleep in so long he'd forgotten what it was like.

Then one morning he rolled out of his bunk, shaking and burning with fever, and with one jaw swelled to the size of a Pecos River cantaloupe. He knew then there was no getting around it; he had to go pay old Doc Fussell a visit.

179

He caught a ride into town on a truck passing the ranch. He climbed the stairs to Doc's office, with those two teeth knocking out a section of his jawbone every heartbeat. He steeled himself for the bigger hurt that was to come with the pulling. But that didn't happen.

Doc took one look at that swollen jaw and balked. He'd pull no teeth out of a jaw in the shape that one was in. Fat would just have to wait till the swelling had gone down.

Fat argued. He told Doc Fussell that he was the one taking the risk. He said if blood poisoning set in, he'd be the one to die, not the doctor. He pointed out that Doc was in the tooth-pulling business, wasn't he? Well, here he'd gone to all this trouble to bring Doc some teeth to pull. It was his money that would pay for it. What right did the Doc have to turn him down?

But his arguments didn't budge Doc Fussell. All the doctor did was grin and ask, "What money?"

Fat's bristles rose. If there's anything a man hates worse than being broke, it's being reminded of it. Fat told him he knew damned well that he'd get paid.

"Ask around if Fat Alford don't pay his debts," Fat invited him. "Just ask anybody."

But Doc wouldn't argue the point. He said he wasn't bothered about the pay. He figured he'd get it when Fat got the money. But that didn't change the picture any. He wouldn't touch those teeth until the swelling went down in that jaw.

Well, there Fat was—string-halted. Done lost a day's wages coming to town, and now Doc wouldn't pull his teeth. Which meant more pain to endure and another trip to town later on and more wages lost.

180

Fat wandered off downtown, hurting from the roots of his hair clear down to his toenails. He squandered a precious nickel on a cup of coffee; it tasted like sheep dip and made him feel sicker and worse broke than ever. He sat and thought about his mother and the kids back there at Christoval. Trying to get along on nothing till he sent them some money; and it'd be a couple of weeks yet before he'd draw any wages.

Dammit, he had to send them some money!

Fat left the coffee counter. He went down the street and hit up Scott Peters, a banker he knew. He told Peters he had to have forty dollars today, right now.

Scott gave him a hard banker's look and asked, "What do you need forty dollars for?"

Fat knew this was a stock question with all bankers everywhere. A lot of them just ask it out of habit, without really meaning to make a man feel as cheap and down at the heel as it always does. Scott had pulled Fat out of a hole more than one time when Fat needed a little money in a hurry. Scott and another Ozona banker by the name of Wayne West had been keeping more than one Depression-broke cowhand from going hungry.

But right then Fat was sore. He'd just lost a day's wages. He'd just lost an argument with Doc Fussell about that tooth pulling. He was sick from the hurt of those teeth and shamed because he had to ask for money to feed his family. So when Scott Peters threw that stock question at him, Fat was suddenly as mad and dangerous as a trapped wild hog.

"Damn it to hell!" he flared. "I don't need that money for nothing—except that old woman that raised me!"

181

He wheeled and headed for the street, with his mind made up. Before he'd beg another banker for a loan, he'd take a gun and pull a stick-up somewhere!

But before he could get through the door, Scott Peters had run out of his cage and tied onto his arm. And now the banker was nearly as sore as Fat.

"Come back in here, you hothead!" Peters shouted at him. "You can have forty dollars or four hundred if you want it. But you don't have to act such a sorehead about it!"

Fat went back and got his forty dollars. And after he'd mailed the money home, he didn't have anything to worry about but his aching teeth.

After suffering three or four more days, he finally got that hurt stopped. He was riding out in the pasture when he happened to feel of his jaw. The swelling had gone down. He felt of his gums. They were softer now, ready to be lanced. He guessed it was time to go back and pay Doc Fussell another visit.

But the way Fat figured it, that would just lose him some more wages and cost him a doctor bill. And out yonder a piece stood a Spanish dagger plant, with blades as sharp-tipped as a doctor's lance and a lot sharper than some. He got out his pocket knife and cut off one of the blades. He trimmed it up, real clean and careful, then ran the point up beside those bad teeth in a way to slice open the gums.

Ten minutes later all the hurt was gone, and Fat was so relaxed and sleepy that he started looking for a place out of the raw wind where he could lie down on the ground in the warm spring sun and sleep for a week.

182

Those Spanish daggers—if a man happens to run the point of one into his leg or some place—they're pretty poison and sometimes make a bad sore. But seems like their poison is just the right sort of medicine to use on an abscessed tooth.

26

AN old-timer, recalling the '17 and '18 drouth in Texas, put it this way, "It just got drier and drier and finally never did rain."

Which pretty well expresses what happened to the ranch country of the whole West during the Depression. Times were bad, year after year, till finally they got worse.

A slightly varied ranch-country joke making the rounds of Texas today had its origin in those years. It tells about two ranch owners sitting down in a café to discuss hard times over a cup of coffee. One says, "If things don't change pretty soon, I'm going to have to go out and rob a bank." At which the other one laughs. "Hell," he says, "if they don't change by the end of this month, I've done got a bank robbed."

Stories of big ranch operators losing a million or so dollars and breaking the banks that supported them were dramatic enough to make newspaper headlines. What those stories didn't tell is what happened to the working cowhand who'd never had a million dollars to lose. After the ranch owner and banker had experienced what for them was utter ruin, nine times out of ten, they were still better off than the working cowhand had been when the Depression started. The rancher and banker still had homes to live in, clothes to wear, and enough to eat.

They weren't like Fat. They weren't reduced to selling the last piece of property they owned to feed their families.

After Fat sold his Model T, his chances for rustling jobs were slimmer than ever. He was broke and sponging off his friends till he was ashamed to face them. He slept and ate mostly at the home of Butch Miller, a little dried-up Ozona butcher, who wasn't much better off financially than Fat, but who did at least have a job.

Finally, a man hired Fat and a boy named Wilson to move a bunch of horses from Boquillas, down on the Rio Grande in the Big Bend country, up to Ozona. He took them down to Boquillas in a pickup, telling them there wasn't any use of bothering with bedding and camping equipment, that he'd meet them at certain watering places, where they'd spend the nights.

However, Fat and Wilson thought it best to take along a sack of flour and a few beans, since this was a cross-country drive, and roads to the camping spots were bad.

As it turned out, this was a lucky move; for, once the horse owner drove away, they didn't see him again until they'd completed the two-hundred-mile drive to Ozona.

They boiled beans in a rusty bucket they found. They made biscuits out of water and flour which they mixed on spread-out leather leggings and cooked by rolling the dough around sticks which they held over the fire. Salt for the beans and biscuits they got from salt troughs ranchers had put out for cattle. The meat they ate was any rabbit or squirrel unfortunate enough to fall before the rocks and clubs they hurled at them.

The weather was cold, with a misty rain falling; and

185

sleeping out in such weather with only their saddle blankets for bedding was not the sort of experience to make a cowhand love his work. After one particularly rough night, during which they'd spent most of their time dragging their short blankets down to cover their freezing feet, then dragging them off their feet to cover their freezing shoulders, Wilson arose in the shivery dawn and gave a bleary-eyed look at the desolate and unfamiliar country about them.

"Dammit!" he swore suddenly. "If I just knowed the way home, I'd quit right here."

Fat shook his head. "No," he said. "After coming this far, I wouldn't quit a-tall. I've always wondered how much a man can stand, and this looks like a good chance to find out."

The two of them stood enough to make it in to Ozona a couple of days later, where the man who'd hired them was terribly sorry about leaving them without grub and bedding like he'd done—only, there hadn't been a thing he could do about it, on account of he'd gotten word that some of his folks were bad sick and he'd been obliged to go see about them.

However, he paid off pretty well, which was what the whole thing had been about, anyhow, as far as Fat was concerned. And by tight-fisting every one of those dollars he could possibly hold onto, Fat had enough to go into the bootlegging business when the next rodeo time came around.

He never had tried bootlegging before, but then he'd never before been so hard up for some means of making a little money. He needed some sort of car to get around in. He needed more money to send home to his family.

The girls were getting bigger now, and were trying to help out at home all they could by gathering pecans and shelling them. They'd got NYA jobs to finance their school supplies. And Bessie had learned to set type for old man Van Horn's newspaper there in Christoval. But, schoolgirls like that, they couldn't earn enough to do any real good. And the last time Fat had been home, he'd caught his mother taking in washing. She hadn't admitted it, but Fat was pretty sure that's what she was doing, and the idea of his mother having to do other people's washing burned him. Fat figured that, by peddling whiskey during this celebration, he could clean up enough to get his mother away from a rubboard, at least.

But, for bootlegging, he needed a car.

Fat went to Butch Miller. "Butch," he said, "if I had me a car, I'd bootleg this round, during the rodeo."

Butch looked at him. "You trying to fight your way into the pen?" he asked.

"I'll have to gamble on that," Fat said. "Right now, I need to get my hands on some money."

And Butch, being a friend instead of a banker, didn't have to ask any more questions; he just told Fat to go ahead and use his car.

Fat lit out for San Angelo, where he inquired around till he'd located a wholesale bootlegger and made a trade with him. He headed back for Ozona after dark, with Butch's car loaded with beer and whiskey till the springs lay flat on the axles. And every time a pair of headlights showed up in the rear-view mirror, he thought about those two federal officers who'd been hanging around Ozona lately, and the hair would start prickling at the back of his neck.

187

But he made it through without getting stopped; and down past Ozona a few miles he took a lease on a cedar grove, just off the highway. The fact that the ranch owner didn't know about it didn't keep it from being a good place; so Fat unloaded the car and got set for business.

The next day was the day before the rodeo started, but folks from far off were already pulling into town. And the drive had been so long and dry that they were needing drinks in a bad way. And after Fat hauled the first customer out to the cedar grove where he had the beer iced down in ten-gallon lard cans and the rotgut whiskey priced at double what he'd paid for it, he didn't have to bother to send a boy around with circulars. The news was already out, and here they came.

Fat did a land-office business that first day and figured to do better the next. But, the first thing the next morning, he ran into Sheriff Sandy Willis.

Fat tried to duck around a street corner before the sheriff saw him, but he was too late. Sandy had already hollered his name and was coming toward him at a fast walk. So Fat stood where he was and commenced getting smaller and closer to the sidewalk every step the sheriff took.

"Fat," Sandy Willis said, "I'm needing a gate deputy at the rodeo. How about helping me out?"

Fat breathed easier, but not a lot. He thanked Willis for offering him the job, then started making excuses. He told Sandy that he'd sort of planned to enter some of the rodeo contests, that he was sure in need of money and he ought to come out with a calf-roping prize, at least.

Sandy stood and listened till Fat had run out of excuses, then looked him straight in the eye. "There's ten dollars in that deputy job, for a couple of hours' work; and I think you'd better take it."

The way Sandy said that gave Fat the feeling that he was being warned. He searched the redheaded sheriff's eyes. But those blue eyes were as sun-baked and alkali-burned as his own; they told him nothing. All Fat had to go by was that strong feeling that Sandy was onto his game and was trying to give him a way out.

On the other hand, knowing Sandy, Fat wasn't real sure but what the sheriff might be thinking what a hell of a joke it'd be to have him working for ten dollars, when he might be making a hundred peddling booze. Sandy was that kind.

How ever it was, Fat would have bet every dollar he'd made the day before that this offer of a deputy's job wasn't just a happen-so.

Fat let the sheriff pin a deputy's badge on his shirt, and there he was, the celebration's chief bootlegger, standing hand in glove with the law.

This was too much for the hooch-guzzling customers he'd sold to the day before. They all gathered around him at the rodeo gate, grinning and looking wise and wanting to know if they had to buy a bottle to get through the gate, or would just a plain ordinary ticket do. They weren't bothering to keep their voices down, either, so that Fat was about half mad and jumpy as a cat on ice by the time the two federal agents came up to him at the gate.

The officers stood close by, eying Fat speculatively

189

till the crowd thinned out a bit. Then they closed in; and Fat's heart dropped down into his boots.

"How about passing us through?" one of them asked. "We're officers of the law."

The letdown was more than Fat could stand. "Dammit!" he flared. "The law ain't no better around here than anybody else. If you want to see this show, you'll buy your tickets, same as other folks."

The officers backed up, looking startled, then turned away. Fat began swearing at himself for being such a fool. But he decided later that this was possibly as good a way as any to have handled the situation. Likely them birds figured that no man with an uneasy conscience would have had the gall to talk to federal agents that way.

Anyhow, they didn't catch onto what everybody else in the country had known since yesterday: that Fat was peddling the juice that was putting all the big whoop and holler into the rodeo.

Fat added the ten dollars he earned by enforcing the law to the several hundred he'd taken in by breaking it, and all of it together was enough to get his mother away from the washpot and to buy him a Model A pickup so he could get around better for job hunting.

Which was sure a relief. After all the scares and anxieties he'd suffered, he decided he'd just about as soon pick cotton for a living as to make it bootlegging.

27

THAT fall, for the first time in seven or eight years of just barely making a living for himself and his family, Fat ran into a streak of luck. That came about when Arthur Phillips hit up Fat and Red Kiser to break some horses at his ranch about twenty-five miles south of Ozona, down in the Juno country. Fat was so glad to be offered any sort of job that he was ready to jump at this one, but Red held off till he could bargain a little. He told Phillips that they'd break the ten horses for him at ten dollars a head if he'd let them hunt and trap for fur on his land while they did it. Phillips saw nothing wrong with that, so the trade was made.

This job turned out to be one of those rare ones that a man can look back on with real pleasure. From start to finish, everything turned out better than Fat could have hoped for.

To begin with, there was Red Kiser, as fine a companion as a man could want. Red was the kind who, if you took a notion you wanted to turn the house over, would pull on his gloves and ask which corner you aimed to start on. Then Oscar Davis, who ran Phillips' ranch for him, put the horsebreakers up in a good tight house, where they could sleep in warm beds at night. This was a real luxury to cowhands who'd spent more of their lives sleeping out on the ground than anywhere else. Then there was wild game for the shooting, and

191

pecans they could pick up and shell; and Oscar even kept them supplied with fresh milk.

They had good tight corrals close by, handy to work the young broncs in; and along the broken-rocks cliffs on the head draws of Devil's River and out on top of the live-oak ridges, they found more fur-bearing animals than a man could believe.

So, during the day, Fat and Red saddled and rode their broncs, taking them in rotation. And Fat showed Red a trick he'd learned for breaking young horses to ride and lead when alone. He'd string three or four of them out, using ropes to tie the head of one horse to the root of the tail of the one in front. Then he'd saddle and mount the one in the lead. And if this lead bronc took the wall-eyed fits, all a man had to do was wave his hat at the others, and they'd fall back against their ropes. Generally, that much pull on his tail was enough to take the fight out of the wildest one a man could get a saddle on.

Then, one night, Red showed Fat a trick he'd learned. He saddled a boogery bronc and got astraddle of him with a spotlight. Every time the bronc took a scare, Red switched the light on. That sudden blinding light in his eyes would bring the wild one out of his spasms just about as quick as Fat's trick would.

When the day's work was done with the broncs, Red and Fat would take to the woods with their rifles and bring down a turkey or deer or maybe a brace of squirrels. Then, after a supper of wild game, when it had got good dark, they'd get out their spotlights and turn loose a couple of varmint dogs Red had brought along and head out down the draws. The dogs would hunt and tree a varmint now and then; but the bulk of the pelts they got by flashing their spotlights along the faces of the rugged cliffs and picking up the reflective lights in the eyes of any animal looking their way. When they'd located a pair of eyes, glowing like live red coals in the darkness, they'd keep the spotlight on them while they walked close enough to make sure what sort of animal it belonged to. Generally, the varmint would hold, staring straight at the light until they got close enough to shoot it.

It was mainly raccoon and ringtails they were after. Raccoon pelts brought a couple of dollars, and ringtails around two and a half. And while hunting them with spotlights was a violation of the game laws, Fat and Red didn't let that worry them any, since they were hunting on land they had permission to hunt on and they knew no game warden was likely to be called in. Sometimes they caught eight or ten furs before they went back to camp to skin their catch and stretch the pelts over boards for drying.

At the end of sixty days of living like kings, Red and Fat wound up their horsebreaking job, collected their hundred dollars from Arthur Phillips, then took their furs to town, where they sold them for eight hundred more.

Making a cleanup like that put ideas into Fat's head. The way he figured it, why should he work his guts out during the cold weather, feeding and tailing up poor cows, when he could make two and three times as much money catching furs—and have more fun doing it?

The fur-catching season for that year was over, but

that didn't keep Fat from making preparations for the next. While he worked here and yonder at his regular cowhand trade, he kept on the lookout for good varmint dogs. But for every good fur-catching dog, there are a hundred sorry ones, and Fat is convinced that he found his full quota of potlikkers before the best hound he ever owned found him.

He was at home, half sick, when E. C. came in one day and told him to come look at a stray hound that was nosing around a pen that held a fair hound bitch Fat had bought off one of the Leifestes at Mason.

E. C. said, "You claim to be a hound-dog man; see what about that one out yonder?"

Fat glanced out the window, then got up to go to the door. In the yard stood as pretty a gyp as he'd ever laid eye on. She was a Walker hound with a brown streak running back from her ears and off down her hind legs. From her stance and the shape of her body, Fat was instantly sure that here was a real hound.

"That's the best hound a-walking," he told E. C. "Go put a collar and chain on her."

"She don't happen to be your dog," E. C. mentioned.

"No," Fat admitted. "But I don't want to see a good hound like that straying off and maybe getting poisoned."

E. C. caught the hound and tied her to a tree. A cold norther was blowing, and Fat got to thinking maybe the dog would get cold; so he hobbled outside and led her around behind the house to get her out of the wind and, incidentally, out of sight.

But it didn't do any good. The next morning an old man drove up to the house and claimed the dog. So

194

there wasn't anything for Fat to do but let her go and swear at himself for not doing a better job of hiding her.

That same afternoon, however, the gyp was back again, smelling around the pen. And when Fat saw her, he got scared all over again that she might get poisoned; this time he put her in the pen with his other dog, Old Pearl, where he was certain she would be out of the weather—and out of sight.

For three or four days afterward, Fat nearly had a relapse, he was so scared the dog's owner would come back for her. But the man didn't show up; and about a week later, Fat got out of bed, ready to go back to work. He opened the dog pen and called Old Pearl out; and when she jumped into the back of the pickup, the gyp followed her—of her own free will and accord. So Fat never did feel that E. C. quite did him justice when he claimed that Fat stole the dog.

Anyhow, Fat took her out to the Massey ranch, where E. C. worked, and where Fat generally kept his dogs. There he learned, to his consternation, that his new dog, which he named Streak, was good for but one thing: she could outrun, fair and square, any jack rabbit that got up ahead of her.

Few hounds are fast enough to perform this feat; but that wasn't much comfort to Fat. What he wanted her for was a coon and ringtail dog, and she sure wouldn't be any good at that, so long as she ran rabbits.

Fat went to work on her, still convinced that he was as good a judge of hounds as he was of horses. He'd hunt with her on horseback, and every time Streak jumped a rabbit, he'd run her down and work her over with the double of his rope. She didn't learn fast, but she learned well; and when Fat finally did convince Streak that running rabbits wasn't a paying proposition, she took to coon and ringtail hunting with the same speed and stubborn tenacity that she'd displayed after rabbits. One night, in a three-hour hunt, she treed fourteen ringtails for Fat. Another time, when he loaned her to E. C. and Charlie Black, she caught them one hundred and ten dollars' worth of fur before daylight. In all the years that he hunted with her before she died, Fat estimates that Streak made him four or five thousand dollars.

If, as E. C. insisted, Fat stole that hound dog Streak, then Fat's convinced there's nothing to that old adage that "crime doesn't pay."

28

UNLIKE most cowhands, who resent a sick spell worse than a five-mile walk, Fat got a certain amount of enjoyment out of his. This was because about the only chance he ever got to visit the family he was having such a struggle to provide for was when he was too sick to work. Also, any time he came home sick, his mother put him to bed and waited on him hand and foot, like a baby; and, to a man not used to having a woman care for him, this sort of attention can be mighty comforting for a change.

However, Fat didn't get much pleasure out of his sick spell the time he was at home and acquired his dog Streak. This was because Cynthia kept after him to hurry up and get well enough to go kill her a jack rabbit. She said she needed it in her schoolwork; that she wanted to boil it till the meat came off the bones.

That sounded crazy to Fat. He told Cynthia that if them teachers had had to eat as many rabbits as he had, they'd know that a cottontail was better meat, and ought to be fried instead of boiled. Cynthia explained that she didn't want to eat the rabbit, that this was her year to take biology and her project in the subject was to boil all the flesh from the bones of some small animal, then take the bones and try to reassemble them—and would Fat hurry and get her one before the time to finish the project was past?

Well, trying to fit the bones of a dead jack rabbit back together sounded to Fat like a lot of nonsense and a devil of a waste of time, but he finally dragged himself out of bed long enough to drive out in his pickup and blow down one of the long-eared animals and bring it home. Then he went back to bed, so his mama could wait on him some more.

But he didn't get to enjoy his mother's attention any time before Cynthia had the jack rabbit boiling in a pot on the back of the kitchen stove, and it smelled so bad that Fat couldn't stand it. He finally had to get up and go fill the big cast-iron washpot out in the yard and build a fire under it. But, even from 'way out there, the scent of that boiling jack rabbit was rank enough to turn his queasy stomach, not to mention how it lured all the neighborhood pot-hounds into the yard. They sat around with drooling jaws, and barked and snapped and wrangled with each other over who was to get the rabbit.

When he couldn't stand the scent and racket any longer, Fat got up and dressed and told his mama that he reckoned he was well. Then he got his stuff loaded together and drove back out to the ranch where he'd been working and piled up in the bunkhouse to enjoy his sick spell in peace and quiet, with nothing worse to smell than some sheep pens and a dipping vat charged with creosote.

The next time he went home, he saw the bleached bones of Cynthia's rabbit lying out on top of a shed roof, and they weren't any better fitted together than he'd thought they'd be.

Which just went to prove what he'd thought from the start: them schoolteachers didn't know nothing!

There for a while, E. C. got to hitting the bottle pretty heavy and running with a tough crowd and getting into a fight now and then. And Fat, who knew where that sort of thing often led, got to feeling it his duty to give his younger brother a little talking-to. He cornered E. C. one day to deliver him a lecture on the evils of drink.

He talked for a good long while, trying to show E. C. that no good could come out of that sort of thing.

"I'll tell you what's going to happen one of these days," he warned. "You're going to be out with the wrong bunch and some damn fool drunk's going to crowd you into killing him or getting killed. And, either way, you're all messed up from then on, with nothing in the world to blame but whiskey."

E. C. sat quiet till he'd heard it all, then proceeded to remind Fat that he was now a grown man, able to take care of himself. He made it plenty plain that if he got into trouble with his drinking, it was his own business and none of Fat's. Then he turned and left Fat standing on the street corner, so hopping mad that he was half a mind to go run E. C. down and give him a good fist whipping for being so mule-headed. But before he did it, Fat got to recollecting that lecture his father had given him years ago about the evils of strong drink and wild women, and how much attention he'd paid to it. That's when he decided that any man handing out advice to people who hadn't asked for it was a complete fool, whether the advice was good or not. He wished

199

that E. C. could understand that whiskey drinking was the same as woman chasing or eating or money-making or anything else a man goes at. A certain amount of it's good for him and adds flavor to living, but, beyond that certain amount, a man's making a hog of himself and asking for trouble. But he guessed E. C. was going to have to learn that through experience, same as he had—about the only way anybody ever seems to learn much.

Having set his own mind straight on the matter, Fat probably would have forgotten the whole thing if E. C. hadn't gone off down the street in a huff and told a couple of friends about this lecture that his big brother was handing out. Which, to anybody who knew how wild Fat had always been, was too much to take lying down. The word got out, and pretty soon half the folks around Ozona were stopping Fat on the streets and grinning, telling him they'd heard he'd turned preacher, and would he give them a little sample sermon? They kept this up till they had Fat about ready to quit the country.

Then one night a couple of Fat's cowhand cronies came to town and invited him to go with them out to a beer joint where they planned to get in some serious drinking. Fat didn't much want to go. He told them that he'd got to where he didn't hardly drink at all any more, but they kept insisting.

"You can drink 7-Up, for all we care," one of them said. "We just want you to go along."

So Fat got in the car with them and they drove out to this beer place just across the line, in a county that voted wet. His cronies ordered beer and Fat ordered

7-Up, and they sat and chewed the rag and were having such an enjoyable time of it that they were still there around midnight when the beer began to take hold of some other long-staying patrons.

One of these was an old boy from town that Fat knew. He sat in a booth close by, with his wife and some others. And the stuff he was drinking must have been the fighting kind, because after a while he came staggering up out of his booth and went over to the bartender and hit him up for a battle.

Well, the bartender didn't want to fight and admitted it, right there before everybody, and wouldn't do a thing but grin when this old boy cussed him for being a coward. So the fighter turned away in disgust and tried to pick a scrap with a customer at the next table. He had no luck there, and finally moved along to grab one of the boys Fat was with by the shoulder and start telling him how tough he was. He invited Fat's friend to take him on for a fight if he thought he was big enough; but Fat's friend was like the others. He knew this old boy was a pretty decent sort when he was sober and he didn't want to have any trouble with him while he was drunk; so he admitted right off that he didn't feel half big enough to fight him.

Wanting to fight as bad as this battler was, and not finding anybody in the house with the guts to fight him, was sure aggravating. He set out then to give everybody in the place a good cussing, telling them just how cheap and sorry the whole bunch was and how he'd just as soon tear this whole joint apart and wipe up the earth with the pieces.

This went on till Fat finally got worn out with listening to it. He picked up a stool and swung it at the drunk's head and laid him out cold on the floor, where he didn't look nearly so tough as he'd been telling around that he was.

Well, of course, the news of Fat's fight in a beer joint was all over town by morning and hadn't lost anything with repeated tellings. E. C. got hold of it and came and wanted Fat to explain how come him so damned pious about whiskey drinking when he'd go out and get drunk and knock a man cold right in the middle of a beer joint.

Fat tried to tell E. C. that he wasn't drunk, that all he'd taken on was a couple or three bottles of 7-Up; but, in a case like this, telling the truth was the worst mistake he could have made. Who was going to believe that a rough and tough cowhand like Fat Alford would sit in a beer joint half the night drinking 7-Up?

Nobody, of course; except old man Tom Casby, who'd been county treasurer at Ozona for nearly always. Old man Tom said he didn't have no reason at all to question the truth of Fat's statement.

"The only thing about it that's got me puzzled," he said, "is why anybody'd drink that old weak, nasty-tasting beer when a good drink like 7-Up packs the wallop it does!"

But Fat sort of got even with E. C. a few weeks later. That was when the two of them piled some steel traps and camping plunder into the back of Fat's pickup and topped off the load with three or four hunting dogs and went down to the Pecos River to camp out awhile and do some coon and ringtail trapping.

By the time they'd gotten there and pitched the camp, the weather had turned off bad. There was a cold, shivery wind blowing out of the east and spitting a little rain.

E. C. had a bad cough going. Fat said it was from smoking too much, and E. C. said it wasn't; so they argued about it while they gathered wood and fixed supper.

Anyhow, it seemed like the weather made E. C.'s cough worse. He got hoarse and kept barking around till the hounds started barking, too, and Fat said maybe they'd better break camp and go in, where E. C. could get some medicine. He said the way the weather had turned off, it didn't look like they'd catch much fur anyhow.

But E. C. wouldn't hear to leaving, and dug around in his camping stuff till he located a bottle of Vicks salve which he rubbed on his chest.

Finally, they both crawled into their camp beds, but E. C. couldn't get any sleep, on account of this deep-seated cough that nearly tore him apart every time it hit him. And Fat couldn't sleep for listening. So after a while, Fat got himself an idea. He got up and dug around in his stuff and came up with a different sort of medicine. He poured about four or five drops into a spoon and told E. C. to take it, that it might help; and E. C., without ever thinking to ask what it was, opened his mouth and swallowed it down and came close to choking to death before he finally got his breath again.

"What in the hell was that?" he demanded.

Fat held the bottle up close to the lantern light and read from the label. "It's called Spahn's Dog Distemper

Medicine," he answered. "It says here that it's good for dogs and cats both."

Right there, E. C. would have whipped a big brother or got whipped if another fit of coughing hadn't brought him to his knees before he could stop it. So he lay down and pacified himself by giving Fat a good cussing before he finally dropped off to sleep.

The next morning, they loaded up their plunder and hounds and drove back home; but that was on account of the weather, and not E. C.'s cough. That distemper medicine Fat had fed him had cured E. C.'s cough completely.

29

WHILE the price of sheep and cattle continued a slow decline, making ranch jobs harder and harder to find, the price of furs went up. Especially the price paid for the pelts of ringtail cats. For a couple of seasons there, the hides of these soft-furred little animals sold for as much as ten dollars apiece.

Fat went more and more to fur hunting during the winter months. With dogs trained to hunt and tree ringtails and raccoons, and with a thorough knowledge of their habitat, gained from working all over that part of the country, Fat could sometimes pick up as much as fifty or sixty dollars' worth of fur in one night. For a while there, he made more money during the fur season than he did all the rest of the year working as a cowhand.

Most of the ranchers knew Fat and readily gave him permission to hunt on their property. But here and there were ranches whose owners tolerated no hunting of any sort. And, of course, it was on these ranches that the raccoons and ringtails were the most plentiful.

One of these was a ranch with headquarters down on Devil's River, between Ozona and Del Rio. Living among the honeycombed limestone cliffs along the river and feeding on the acorns and pecans that grew in the canyon valley were coons and ringtails in numbers al-

205

most unbelievable. And, to Fat, who made some of his best catches on this posted property, it seemed like there was a game warden for every acre of land.

Fat puts the blame for poaching on this property on the shoulders of his friend Allen Watson. Allen was a Negro cowhand who'd been forced out of work by hard times and was now shining shoes in one of the local barbershops. When fur prices went up, Allen couldn't help recollecting how thick the coons and ringtails had been down on Devil's River when he'd worked there years before, and how easy it would be to pick up some much-needed cash if he could get permission to fur hunt there for a while.

Well, he couldn't get permission; so he came to Fat with a proposition. He knew every foot of the country; so how about their teaming up and slipping in there at night?

The idea scared Fat at first. "Why, Allen," he said, "that's a hornets' nest down there. They ever catch us, we'll be in that Del Rio jail from now on!"

"I know," Allen said, "but we can kill more coons and ringtails along that river than we can pack off."

Fat hedged a little longer, but what Allen proposed looked too good. Not only did they stand a chance of making some good money, but look what sport they'd have, trespassing on posted property and maybe getting away with it. That part appealed to Fat almost as much as the money.

They talked it over and made their plans. They left Ozona one night after dark, taking with them a third man to drive the pickup. They couldn't afford to leave

206

the car where some game warden might spot it. They took no dogs; just their guns and spotlights.

They followed the Del Rio-Ozona highway till they came to a shallow draw just opposite the ranch headquarters. Here, the driver slowed as if being cautious about the culvert he had to cross, and before he'd picked up speed again, Fat and Allen had quit the pickup and were running through the darkness toward a patch of brush that would give them cover.

They climbed quietly over the wire fence, then headed downriver. Once they figured they were far enough away from the ranch headquarters that their lights wouldn't show, they turned them on and began searching the cliff faces and the branches of the trees.

It was like Allen had predicted; there were coons and ringtails everywhere. Mostly they were in the pecan groves, feeding on the nuts that littered the ground. Some were up in the trees. Any direction he threw the light, Fat could pick up the eyes of the feeding animals.

Allen did the shooting. Allen was the best night shot with a .22 rifle that Fat ever encountered. Fat would pick up a pair of eyes with his light and, almost before he could steady it, Allen's gun would crack and out would tumble a coon or ringtail, shot squarely between the eyes.

They shot and gathered the animals till the loads became heavier than they could carry. Then they picked out piles of driftwood and patches of brush to hide them in, and went on hunting.

Well, it wasn't long till here came the game wardens. Fat heard the clatter of hoofs among the rocks and shut off his light.

"We better get high behind, Allen," he said.

They took off down the river in a hard run, stumbling over unseen rocks and drifts. Suddenly Allen grabbed Fat's arm and whispered, "Hold it, Fat!" They stopped, and, sure enough, here came the sound of a second rider, from downstream.

Fat took a quick look around. To their left was the river; to their right, a cliff too high and sheer to climb. They were hemmed in.

"Looks like it's the river for us, Allen," he said.

They were standing on a high bank, and just under them was what looked like to Fat in the darkness a broad sand bar. He leaped off and found that it wasn't sand at all, but a deep pool of still water.

It was a frosty night and the shock of that chill water closing over his warm body paralyzed Fat for a moment. He sank down and down and down, unable to move a muscle that might have checked his descent. Finally, he started back up without ever having touched bottom, then began struggling. At last, just when he knew he couldn't hold his breath an instant longer, his head shot above the surface. But if it hadn't been for Allen, who scrambled down to help him, Fat doubts that his chill-shocked muscles would ever have functioned in time to save him from drowning.

Allen pulled him to safety, whispering, "My goodness gracious, Fat. What ever made you do that?"

Fat was too cold to answer.

Allen led and half dragged him over the rocks and ledges to where there was a sand bar. Fat lumbered across it behind Allen, his boots squirting water at every step, his drenched clothes slopping about him.

When they came to the water again, it was at a shallower place, where the stream flowed across a gravel bar.

Allen started in, but Fat pulled him back. "No use in your getting wet, too," he said. "Climb on my shoulders."

Allen climbed on Fat's shoulders and Fat stumbled through waist-deep water to the other side, where they tore out in a hard run across a smooth gravel bar better than three hundred yards wide. They still hadn't quite made it to cover when the lights of the two game wardens reached out across the river after them. But neither light had quite centered on the hunters before they were out of the open and into the brush again.

Fat thought he'd freeze to death that night while he waited around in the cold for the game wardens to leave so they could sneak back across the river and round up their catch.

Luckily, they didn't have to wait too long beside the highway before their driver came back and picked them up. But it was long enough for one of the game wardens to get wise and come out searching for them in a car. He followed them for a while, but the driver Fat and Allen had at the wheel was a good one, and after about a forty-mile chase, the game warden gave it up.

The next morning when they went out to unload their pickup and skin their catch, they found that they'd made better than fifty dollars apiece on that night's run.

After that, Fat and Allen went back several times, making a good catch every night. But finally the game wardens got so hot after them that they couldn't get time to hunt; they were too busy running and dodging. Anyhow, the fun of outwitting those game wardens had sort of worn off, so they finally quit and went back to hunting where they had permission to go.

30

IF this were a fiction story, it would tell how Fat fought courageously through the Depression, went back to cow work, fell in love with the boss's daughter, and married himself a ranch to live on happily ever after.

Begin a story of fact, it doesn't wind up quite like that.

Fat fought through the hard years the best he knew how, working when he could get work, fur hunting in season, deer hunting for meat in and out of season, now and then wild-hog hunting down in the canyon country near the mouth of the Pecos. The butchered hogs he sometimes ate, more often sold to the Mexican population of Ozona, who were glad to get cheap meat, regardless of quality. He rode the Rio Grande for one year as a river guard for the State Sanitary Board, to prevent the crossing of Mexico cattle that might be carrying the dread hoof and mouth disease. He even spent a few months working as an oil-field roustabout. He did any and everything to provide a living for himself and his mother and younger sisters. And while there were times when that living was a pretty meager one for them all, still none of them ever went naked or hungry.

When the approach of World War II put new life

into the livestock business again, Fat went back to work at the trade he'd followed since he was sixteen years old. By this time, the girls at home had grown up and married, leaving him with only his mother to support. This lessened considerably the constant drain on his income; but, by this time, a number of marked changes had taken place in the ranching business. To begin with, the big pastures were being cut up into smaller ones, eliminating almost completely the big spring and fall roundups. On top of that, sheep and cattle were no longer being driven to market. Now, they were being hauled from ranch to railhead by huge trailer trucks that could save days in time and hundreds of pounds of valuable meat through speedy transportation.

And then there was the change-over from cattle to sheep. That trend had started several years before, due partly to the Depression, but mostly to the fact that overgrazing had stripped the ranges of grass till cattle grazing was no longer profitable. So sheep, having the ability to put on fat where grass is so short that a cow will starve, were brought in to clip the grass shorter. What the ranchmen plan to do when the sheep have close-cropped their grass till it dies completely is a question that Fat has no answer for.

That, however, is the landowner's problem, not Fat's. Fat's concern as a working cowhand had to do with the coming of the wetback Mexican, who slipped across the Rio Grande and gladly took over the working of sheep at half the pay the regular cowhand drew.

At first, like most of his kind, Fat resented the wetback's usurping his job. To him, it looked like Mexico was retaking Texas without ever firing a shot. Later, after he'd had a chance to talk with several of these Mexicans, his attitude toward them began to change. Starving to death in his own country, the Mexican couldn't be expected to stay there and submit to it when he could draw wages that were fabulous, comparatively speaking, in Texas. Fat had known enough rough times in his life to understand that.

But understanding an economic problem doesn't necessarily solve it, as Fat quickly learned when he went back to ranch work. With the army draft draining the country of men, there were plenty of jobs open to him. But at every ranch, the situation was the same: he found himself about the only experienced man on the job, the rest of the crew consisting mainly of high-school kids and wetback Mexicans. And while the Mexicans were usually willing enough to work, they knew too little about it; and with the high-school kids, it was generally a case of their liking the idea of working as cowhands a lot more than they really liked the work.

As a result of this situation, the ranch owners invariably depended on Fat to see that the work was done right. Which would have been fair enough, except that there was no extra pay, and the fact that he had so little help. In most cases, neither the kids nor the Mexicans could handle a rope, shoe a horse, ride a fractious mount, or even pen a bunch of sheep if they happened to take a scare. Which left Fat trying to oversee a job that one time had required the help of eight or ten experienced cowhands, then finally having to do most of the actual work himself.

Fat stayed with it awhile; but finally his patience wore thin. The ranch owners were making enough money now to have paid an experienced man good wages. And while wages paid to their hired help was deductible from the high income taxes they paid, it seemed like they'd much rather pass it along to Uncle Sam than sweeten the pot for their hired help. It didn't make sense to Fat, but that's the way it was.

Finally, like his friend Howard Capps had done at the edge of the mesquite thicket on the Pecos, Fat sat down and had a little talk with himself. And, as a result of that conversation, he sacked his saddle, coiled his rope, and headed for town. There, he first tried to join the U. S. Marines, figuring that, with the nation at war, one extra man might mean the difference between winning and losing it. But his age and a potbelly stopped him there, so he studied awhile, then traded for a truck. With it, he began hauling cow feed from the farms to the ranches, and livestock from the ranches to the auction rings and shipping pens. He found that, for a man of his age, hauling livestock in a truck was a whole lot easier than working it from the back of a horse, not to mention the fact that the truck made him three times as much money as he'd ever made working as a cowhand.

That's when a dream he'd packed around in the back of his mind for years began to push to the front. Why not start putting up some of this hauling money and buy himself a ranch of his own?

The odds were all against it, of course. To begin with, Fat wasn't as young as he'd once been. On top of that, now that livestock had become more valuable than ever before in the history of the nation, the price of good ranch land was soaring sky-high, far beyond the ordinary man's ability to pay. And, to cap it all off, the government's drift toward a welfare state—which to Fat's way of thinking means taking money from a man who'll work and giving it to a man who won't—was clipping his income till it looked about half silly even to hope to accumulate anything above a bare living.

Still, what are long odds to a working cowhand? Long odds are all that most of them ever know. Yet look at Fat's friend, Abe Caruthers, who for years worked as a bronc-peeler for the Montague outfit. Abe started out like Fat, with nothing but an old hull of a saddle and a lot of fight to him. And now Abe owned some forty sections of good land and had his family housed in as fine a home as there was in Ozona.

Abe would be the first to admit that he'd gotten a lucky break, the Montagues being one of the few ranch outfits of West Texas that would give a working man a chance to better himself. But maybe, Fat told himself, he'd get a lucky break along the line somewhere, too. He'd had plenty of the other kind.

By nature, cowhands are the sort who'll bank strong on their luck. Fat went to work with his truck, hauling for pay, swapping horses and cows, buying cow feed here and selling it there. Crowding his luck for all it was worth.

Today he owns that ranch. It's not the ranch he still dreams about. It's too small. There are only five sections of it, lying out a piece from Wildhorse Springs, New Mexico; and five sections is not nearly enough room for a cowhand who has seen the time when he could ride straight ahead from sunup to sunset and still be on the same ranch. And it's piñon country, where it's too high and too cold, so that the summer grazing

215

period is too short and the winter snows lie on the ground too long. But it's a start. It's a toehold. It's one foot set solid in the stirrup.

And one foot in the stirrup is all an experienced cowhand ever asks of a bronc he's fixing to step across.

F 84